Everybody Needs Somebody

By

M.J. Boyle

Copyright © *M.J. Boyle,* 2024
All Rights Reserved

The right of M.J. Boyle to be identified as author of this work has been asserted by the author in accordance with sections 77 and 78 of the Copyright, Designs and Patents Act 1988.

All rights reserved. No part of this publication may be reproduced, stored in a retrieval system, or transmitted in any form or by any means, electronic, mechanical, photocopying, recording, or otherwise, without prior permission of the publishers/the author.

Any person who commits any unauthorised act in relation to this publication may be liable to criminal prosecution and civil claims for damages.

This is a work of fiction. Names, characters, businesses, places,events,locales, and incidents are either the products of the author`s imagination or used in a ficticious manner. Any resemblance to actual persons, living or dead, or actual events is purely coincidental.

A CIP catalogue record for this title is available from the British Library.

Paperback ISBN: 978-1-83663-022-7

"It is amazing what you can do with your imagination."

*In memory of the countless times I watched
"Charlie Bear" with my grandchildren Mia, Philina, & Marlon.*

Introduction

Just for the hell of it, let's consider life as a cookery course where we all create our individual recipes.

Let's stand back and take a look at life - our own, and maybe how it is affecting others', and other people's, and how theirs are influencing ours – we see that there are parallels between that and cooking. Puzzled? Read on

Cooking is not everyone's cup of tea. But it is something that more-or-less everyone comes into contact with at some point in their life.

For some, it will remain a task to be avoided as far as possible, for others it will develop into a hobby.

For the huge amount of people in between those two groups, it is a constant companion with very, probably, differing feelings along the way. It all depends on who you are cooking for, how many you are cooking for, how often you have to cook, how much time you have for the task and, not least, how much money you have to spend.

Isn't that just like life? The perceived quality of one's life also depends on who you are sharing your life with, how many you are sharing your life with, how often you have quality time together, and, not least, on whether you have money worries or not.

One can cook according to a recipe from a cookery book, or from memory, search for new ideas, earth out some old family recipes, or simply experiment.

One chooses the style of cooking, the seasoning, the side dishes – and the setting. Should one sit in the armchair in front of the television, eat in the kitchen, or set the dining room table?

Whether our lives are easy, difficult, well-seasoned, or bland, it is up to each and every one of us to make a life for ourselves. A life that we actually want, enjoy, and even relish. There seems, however, to be one particular aspect of life which is of implicit complexity and can turn life upside down – communication, or more precisely, the lack of it.

How often does life serve us a situation in which we feel it would be impolite, or at least, not beneficial to the situation, to really express what we feel. Whatever the language, there is such a vast spectrum of words at our disposal, yet we stick to old patterns we know best and thus allow ample scope for misunderstandings and misinterpretations. As listeners, we also play along and, with no questions asked, allow abundant leverage for our own assumptions.

Everything starts with a given – let`s take beef, for example. Sometimes, we have a steak, sometimes a joint, and sometimes mince.

So, just to prove a point: if life has (even temporarily) made minced meat of us, we still have plenty of choices open to us.

We choose our recipe and make the best of it.

PART 1:

Minced Meat as Food for Thought

Janice

"Damn, I've forgotten the salt!" she had exclaimed as she put the shopping into the back of the car. Truth be known, she hated grocery shopping and had always made excuses as to why she shouldn't be the one to have to do it. Now though, there was no-one to listen to the excuses. He had just upped and left – after all those years. Gone, leaving behind what he now considered a waste of time, time that he claimed he no longer had to offer.

Well, now she had to find time for all sorts of things.

He had gracefully offered to leave her the house, a car and the hot tub in the garden. It was just him she would have to do without from now on. He had given an obviously well-rehearsed speech which had been delivered, for her at least, out-of-the-blue just two Sundays ago.

Even the shattered look on the face of their eight-year-old son couldn't stop him from leaving

She was, however, well-pleased with herself that she had managed to calm herself down and was about to tackle the future with poise. About to, because poise was admittedly missing at present. The telephone call with Tim hadn't gone too well yesterday evening, certainly not as she had planned it. She'd spent two full hours preparing her points and anticipating his responses, then mulling over her intended reactions to his anticipated reactions. She had carefully explained why it was important that he should remain a stable part of Dylan's life. That she had no intention of jeopardizing their relationship, in spite of everything. Once that was out, he had pounced on the "in spite of everything," like a tiger that had been waiting for ages for this opportunity to come along, executed like an ambush and followed by an onslaught over how she was obviously in denial of what had happened, in fact, more of, what hadn't happened in their long relationship.

The conversation didn't improve when she asked about how he thought the financial situation should be settled. She tried to be sensible, tried to sound grown-up and understanding. It took all the courage she had to admit that actually she couldn`t manage on her wage alone, even if he had left her the house, a car and the hot-tub in the garden. He threatened to have future conversations only with a lawyer present – how on earth was she going to be able to pit against that? Through some stroke of luck, he had received a message from some senior executive from work during the conversation and had to round up rather more quickly than planned. As a result of which, Dylan would now be with him every second weekend and every Wednesday afternoon from 4.00pm – 9.00pm (incl. a sleep-over, whenever possible on his side). The financial question could not be brushed away so easily. That was postponed for a later date.

How come she had never realized what kind of person she was living with? How come she had only ever seen the successful, jovial, (OK – rich), practical, reliable, clever, person with whom she had shared the last ten years?

She sat down – initially to feel sorry for herself – with a bottle of white wine in front of her and an empty glass in her hand. She was hit by a feeling so intense that she set the glass down with a thump. Drinking was now out of the question, she had to have her wits about her.

All those adjectives she so readily found to describe the person she thought she loved, and not one within throwing distance of caring, loving, compassionate, sexy.

What had gone wrong? When did it go wrong? And most importantly, how come she had never noticed?

It would be too easy to blame Dylan, although he was a difficult child to contend with. If it had been someone else`s child, she might even have gone so far as to say he was a typical child from a one child family. Spoilt and full of himself. She had plenty of those in the County Education Office every week. Although as a junior clerk, she fortunately didn`t have to make any fundamental decisions, she certainly saw plenty of messy situations involving children.

She realized she was slightly off track already - she couldn't make it Dylan's fault.

Maybe the white wine was a good idea, after all. Let's not forget, it was a Pouilly Fumè. Tim wouldn't miss it. Above all, it would make thinking of the "in-laws" easier. They must be having a ball by now. They had always said she wasn't good enough for their son. They were probably the ones behind the fact that he had never proposed to her. They had never once talked about getting married. How come that had never occurred to her before? They had talked about all sorts of other things. About holiday destinations, Dylan's teachers, plants in the garden, Dylan's tennis trainer, the new furniture, Dylan's school equipment, the local council meetings, Dylan's sprained ankle, even about Tim's Mum's health problems.

Come to think of it, *when did we ever talk about us?* She considered this in disbelief.

Us, as a pair. Us, as lovers. Us, as people. People with feelings. Feelings that can get hurt. Feelings that hurt so much they feel like they won't ever heal.

Tomorrow is the first day of the rest of your life, she thought as she went to bed. Alone and miserable.

Having forgotten to buy the salt, their evening meal had been bland, to say the least, although even with salt, she probably would have messed it up. This wasn't lost on Dylan, and he plainly told her so. "When Daddy cooked the meals, they always tasted absolutely super. Surely, it is not that difficult."

This was going to be another long and exhausting evening. Dylan was hell-bent on making her life difficult now. So anti. So obnoxious.

She hadn't anything to say that he wanted to hear. Another bottle of Pouilly Fumè?

No, internet first. There must be something out there – something to do on Wednesday evenings. As of next Wednesday. No hanging about.

The choice was not quite as comprehensive as she had hoped, but all in all, when she stared at the screen and saw the confirmation of her registration, she was actually quite pleased with herself.

Community Centre – every Wednesday, starting next week – a basic cookery course run by a local teacher – the course on offer was going to be all about cooking minced meat – all six evenings of it!

Just four weeks ago, she wouldn't have considered it for a second. Now it seemed like the answer to at least two of her current issues.

Well, the first day of the rest of her life came, as it had to. She got up, woke Dylan up, made breakfast, got Dylan off to school on time, showered, got dressed and got herself off to work on time. The daily routine at work engulfed her all day, so much so that she forgot to take her lunch break. At least that is what she told her colleagues; the truth was, she couldn't face their questions. It became obvious that, as she had foreseen the evening before, her fresh start was going to have to be beyond the boundaries of the council offices.

With Dylan at his father's for his first sleep-over, she headed off to the Community Centre. Parked the car in the nearby car park and walked the remaining two hundred yards with a slightly uneasy feeling in her stomach. As she reached the bottom of the steps leading up to the main entrance, she suddenly noticed a familiar face, also aiming for the steps. An old school friend. Well, actually more a girl that had gone to the same school, same time as her. It was, yes, it was definitely – Lavinia.

Lavinia

What is Lavinia doing here?

"Cheers!" they had all said in unison, "Congratulations!"

She had been waiting for ten long months for this day to arrive, and there it was, in all its glory. She had been promoted. She was the "Team Leader." Next step on the ladder had successfully been accomplished.

She had worked hard for it, she was certainly entitled to it.

She had been the best candidate, had the best qualifications, and had the best performance record. It would mean more responsibility, more money and possibly, more hours, but it was worth it.

Her only hope was that her family would be as delighted as she was.

On the way home, she had stopped off at the supermarket and bought some champagne (for her and Ian) and some non-alcoholic, sweet, bubbly stuff (for George and Chelsey). Hardly through the front door, she realized she maybe shouldn`t have bothered. Quite obviously things were not all well in the household. There was shouting to be heard from Chelsey`s bedroom upstairs, seemingly something to do with the fact she had the worst, most unbearable, insensitive brother imaginable. In response, George explained that he could hardly be blamed for the situation, for it was indeed her fault for being self-centred and utterly insane. No calming voice of the father to be heard. She considered pretending she hadn`t yet arrived, but only for a split second. Then let out a roaring "I`m home!" This was unfortunately not heard. So, she climbed the stairs and repeated it as calmly as possible, which actually did not sound very calm at all considering the powerful volume necessary. It did have the desired effect, though. They both shut up.

She went back downstairs to the kitchen to start preparing the dinner.

Ian arrived ten minutes later, he`d nipped out to the Chinese take-away and the off-license to get dinner and some bubbly to celebrate. He had been given an unexpected promotion. It would mean more responsibility, more money, and, of course, more hours, but it was worth it. He was delighted. The children were also delighted - to have Chinese in the middle of the week and had no complaints about being allowed a sip of real champagne.

After they had gone up to their respective bedrooms, Ian walked into the lounge with the second bottle of champagne. He couldn`t understand how he hadn`t noticed it in the fridge before; must have been left over from the last party. Never mind, they`d open it and work out how they would manage the family timetabling changes which, naturally, would now be necessary. He thought Lavinia could reduce her working load, maybe to 50%. They could well afford it now. How good life was. Cheers!

She had said nothing, nothing about her buying the second bottle, no mention of her promotion, not a word about her possible extra hours, and certainly nothing about her in no way wanting to reduce to 50%

She just said "Cheers!" over and over, it seemed.

Next morning, once showered and seemingly sober, she resigned herself to the fact that resistance would be meaningless. Mutiny was not an option. She went through all the motions. She went off to work, outwardly her normal self. No one noticed any difference. Inwardly, she was disappointed, sad, and, yes, angry. Angry with Ian, with what life was throwing at her and somewhere down the line, angry with herself. She could have said something, could have discussed the issues involved. Could actually even have just told Ian that she, too, had received a promotion. He knew, didn`t he? - that she had been waiting for it. But she figured it wasn`t worth the trouble it would cause – without actually knowing what trouble it would cause. She wouldn`t know because she wouldn`t do anything because she never had. She was reconciled to the fact that she was merely a sideshow.

By lunchtime, she was in a really foul mood, so much so that everyone was avoiding her. The male co-workers thought it must be pre- or post-menstrual, the female co-workers thought it must be hiccups on cloud nine.

By closing time, she had written to head office to tell them that she was grateful for the opportunity they were offering, and greatly appreciated the confidence they were showing in her, but that she could not accept the new position.

She remained in the office for an extra hour. An hour she used to good purpose. She searched and found an outlet for her rebellion. The Community Centre – on offer was a basic cooking course; six evenings about cooking with minced meat. Starting next Wednesday. Perfect. Wednesday was one of the busiest days for extracurricular activities, for the children, and for Ian. That would show them at home that she was not purely there to dance attendance on them. The confirmation of the registration came through, and she went home feeling superbly defiant.

Wednesday came, and she headed off for the Community Centre in the middle of town after a rather heated discussion at home about whose turn it was to clear up after dinner and why she could no longer accept the responsibility every Wednesday. She parked her car in the supermarket car park and walked the rest of the distance with an unease which she found hard to understand. As she approached the steps that led up to the main entrance, she recognized a familiar face from school – it was, what was her name again? Oh yes, Janice.

Rather stiff hellos and questions about one`s well-being that actually neither really wanted to be answered anyway were exchanged. It took a mere two minutes for them to realize that they were actually both headed for the same place. They paced up the steps, basking in new-found togetherness.

Once inside the building they looked for the display cabinet announcing where exactly they had to go. Standing in front of it, they were joined by a third person, obviously equally at a loss as to where he had to go.

They both turned around and were faced with a young man in his mid-twenties.

Andrew

Who is this young man?

"Not again!" he had screamed out loud, slamming the lid of the laptop down. He wasn't sure how much more he could take of this. This was his umpteenth application refusal this month alone. His mother would have a field day if she knew. She had told him right from the start, "Oceanology is not your future."

He heard the slam of the door of the flat next to his. Must be 3.15, then – she's off to pick up the kids from school - you don't need clocks in flats like this, with neighbours like his. Everyone seemed to have a routine, the same things done at the same time, day in, day out. Leaving for work, returning from work. Showering, listening to the news, having sex, and even arguing with spouses, or partners, seemed to have a certain time schedule.

Oh, how he would love to be part of such a world.

Not even his working timetable had any resemblance to routine; if they called him, he'd go in, if they didn't, he wouldn't. If he went in, he'd get paid; if he didn't, he wouldn't. Simple – but not what he wanted.

He knew that now.

He hadn't ever really enjoyed school. It had always been more of a compulsory exercise. Other exercises, such as sports, weren't really high up on his list of things he couldn't wait to do, either. He'd visited the local youth club every now and again and had often completed an otherwise incomplete team playing something or other, but that was basically it. He enjoyed swimming, though. He was quite good at it. Had almost made the school team.

Almost, but not quite. Like so many other things in this life.

He had almost, but not quite, managed to hold on to that wonderful female creature he had dated at university.

He had almost, but not quite, achieved a first-class honours degree.

He had almost, but not quite, got any of the jobs he had applied for over the past few months.

What he did get was a job at the DIY store in this mid-England town, a zero-hours contract, which was so precarious it was untrue. Under normal circumstances, he wouldn't have managed to secure a flat with these kinds of credentials, but – and here he had been lucky – one of his uni pals was on a six-month trip around South America and had not wanted to give up his lease on this flat, so he had allowed him to move in for the period of his absence. Here, his luck ended, though.

No job on the horizon and no girlfriend on the horizon, either. One-night stands, which ended up in one-morning embarrassments, were as far as he had got in the "love" section of life recently. It seemed that no one, no female person, was really interested in what he had to say about marine world problems. This made easy conversation difficult because it was actually the only topic he felt at ease with. Maybe he should go back to university after all. They had said right from the start – this should be seen as a basic course. Any career in this field will definitely involve a Masters, or even a PhD.

There were so many job adverts around that simply said that a degree was necessary. The subject didn't seem to matter. Obviously, it was more important that one had proven oneself to have enough personal discipline to get through the three years of academia than to have actually studied a topic remotely associated with the work one was to do later. Except, of course, if one had studied oceanology. Then it was suddenly almost, but not quite right.

He concluded – after his third Hobgoblin beer of the evening – that he needed some kind of interest, some kind of hobby. In fact, something to do on at least one of the evenings he was not down the pub, something that he could talk to other human creatures about.

So, Friday, Saturday & Sunday are out. Still leaves, Monday – Thursday. There must be something out there. Something unusual, something that not every other guy in the pub knew more about. Something that would make him, at least a little, interesting.

If that were not possible, then something that would entail him being in a group with predominantly women – yes, that would do for starters. He could take things from there.

Let`s think: Cars – petrol; university – learning; pub – beer; women – cooking.

Yes, that`s it. Something to do with cooking. Couldn`t be expensive, though. That was definitely a huge hurdle to overcome. He certainly didn`t want to go so far as to forgo any of this drinking money for this journey into the unknown.

So, Community Centre? Possibly.

Wednesday, there was a basic cookery course which started next Wednesday. The course on offer was about cooking with minced meat. Oh my God!! How could he even be considering this?

It must have been the three beers which guided him to the registration form and helped him fill in the particulars. It was certainly the beers, and only the beers which were pleased when the confirmation of registration arrived on the screen.

He`d registered, so he would see this through.

Wednesday arrived, he was called in for a full six-hour shift. Wednesday evening arrived, and he walked across town to the Community Centre. Up the steps to the main entrance. Over to the display unit. Where the hell did he have to go?

He found help in the form of two women who were also standing at the display unit. They were also registered in the course. Well, OK, they were slightly older than him and definitely not his type – *did he have a type?* He asked himself.

Off they walked together towards the allocated room.

Standing outside the door, looking slightly lost, or maybe it was more undecided than lost, was a young woman Andrew thought he recognized from somewhere; just couldn`t figure out where. As they drew closer, he realized it was Tina. Tag-along Tina.

Tina

Why is Tina here?

"Yes, Dad. 5 o´clock, as always," she had sighed into the telephone. As if she had anywhere else to go after work.

It wasn`t that she didn`t love her parents, but she was beginning to feel suffocated by their close proximity. No, not beginning - this had been building up for a long time. She just hadn`t wanted to admit it. Neither to herself, nor to her parents. Something had to change. Quickly.

Work was OK, maybe that was part of the problem. It was only 'OK', but it had been her choice. It had been what she had wanted. Had wanted. Now she wasn`t so sure that this was the life she really felt was hers forever. Where, and indeed how, should she start the 'big shift'?

With a steady job at the bank and a well-stuffed savings bank account to her name, it shouldn`t be too difficult to find a flat to rent (or even buy?) and to buy some furniture. She checked the internet and noted the address and telephone number of the local estate agents who specialized in rental property. It was possibly too early to be considering buying. No, it wasn`t a deja vu, it was pure hypocrisy. She had done this so many times already that she knew the details off-by-heart. She had actually already stood in front of the show window (three times to be precise) but never managed to go inside. Every single time, she saw with her inner eye the looks on the faces of her parents. They would simply not understand. They would assume she no longer appreciated what they had done and were doing for her. They would think she wanted to break-away.

Well, that part was true. She did. It was not a pure and simple escape from them and their presence, though. It was more fleeing from the reality of what her life was and how much it differed from what she felt she really wanted. Probably, if she had a steady boyfriend, things would be a lot easier. They would probably accept that she would move out to start a family life. No such luck. Every boyfriend she had ever had was short-lived and never got as far as meeting her parents. So, they never got so far as to realize that she'd even had any boyfriends.

There were obvious advantages in living with them. She didn't have to worry about her laundry. Her mother dealt with that. She didn't have to worry about maintaining the car, or cleaning it, or even filling it up, her father managed that. She didn't have to clean the bathroom (although it was for her use only), her mother handled that. She didn't have to bother with the garden, her father attended to that (she just enjoyed the peace and relaxation she found in the hammock between the trees at the end of the lawn). She didn't even have to worry about meals, her mother delighted in the

preparation of those. She cooked a meal for them all every evening. At 6 o'clock on the dot, it was on the table. Life was, seen like this, almost perfect. Almost perfect, almost.

So, at almost 29, she had the almost perfect life, and so, why should she want to rattle any chains? Probably because that "almost 29" would be over in just six weeks and would be followed by "heading for 30," and by 30, she needed to have achieved a nigh-on perfect life, at least. The difficulty would be manoeuvring everything into place without upsetting the cart in the meantime. Moving out would probably prove the biggest shift, although finding a life partner could presently be considered daunting – that would have to be left to fate. He would, of course, then do all things her father did for her. So, pragmatic thinking led her to the conclusion that her best start would be in ensuring she could do all the things her mother now did for her. Laundry – the washing machine came with a manual, so no foreseeable problem there. Cleaning – couldn't nigh-on anyone manage that? Cooking – there is the problem. So, there must be the start. The start of the "big shift" - postpone the real planning phase to a later. Procrastination of the purest sort.

She turned on the computer in search of cookery classes. The offerings were extensive, but once she focused on the important issues: must be local, cheap, after work, and, of course, must be for beginners, the choice was narrowed down immensely. In fact, the only course that hadn't yet started and still had free places was at the Community Centre.

Since when did they offer cookery classes? Heavens: basic cookery course where one could register for a specific six-week block. The six-week block starting now was all about minced meat. It wasn't quite the big bang effect she had envisaged for her first step in the direction of the "big shift," but she still felt happy to press the button and submit her registration. Within seconds the computer announced she had been successful and could participate.

So, here she stood at the entrance to the kitchen. She took a deep breath and opened the door. Behind her, she could hear the voices of a group of people, obviously still searching for their room. In front of her, she saw a familiar face. It was the receptionist from the doctor's surgery. She remembered her name because it was the same as her sister-in-law's: Heather.

Heather

How does Heather fit in?

"I promise to do my best to be there," she said, and she had meant it when she said it. Things weren't as easy for her as they were for him. He didn't have a spouse at home to whom he would have to explain his absence. She did. He didn't have any children at home any more. She did have children (or rather child – she had only the one daughter) waiting for her, even expecting attention when Mummy came home.

She did feel drawn towards him, but did she really love him? Love him enough to give up everything she had in their modern semi in a quiet cul-de-sac in the suburbs of the town?

He did, of course, have something to offer in return. A large house with three reception rooms, plenty of money in the bank, and a fine reputation as a competent and popular GP. A place in the upper realms of the local community.

And, he did seem to have fallen for her.

It had started so unexpectedly - at least for her. He was her boss and she had respected, indeed really liked him. She enjoyed working with him. He was so charming, and he had often told her how well he thought she was running his surgery. How smooth everything was going now that she was in charge. Then came the day when he had said he was going to increase her salary. As recognition of her efforts and obvious talents; organizing his appointments and bonding with his patients.

She had stayed on after the other nurses had left because he had said he had something to tell her. When she entered the staff lounge, he was there with a bottle of champagne and a sheet of paper in his hand. She was thrilled that she should be so appreciated. This was something new for her. She took the paper he offered, it was her new contract, which was to be valid as of next month. They drank the champagne and talked and talked. It was so easy to talk to him. He had a certain way with him that made one feel instantly at ease. After the second bottle had been opened, they talked about more personal things. He was a widower, and his children were both at university; these facts she already knew. He was interested in theatre and music, this she had heard. He felt abandoned, and he was lonely; this was new.

She had been married to Jack for eight years, and they had a daughter, Emily, aged six; as her employer, he already knew this. She was interested in music and gardening, he noticed the similarity to his late wife. She felt smothered, and she was lonely, this made his heart melt.

And now, three months on, they were secret lovers. Hiding their feelings – or at least they thought so – and stealing time for each other.

Her biggest problem was that the smallness, the compactness of her family, meant that they all spent a lot of time with each other and basically knew exactly what each was doing at any specific time. Apart from the daughter's weekly ballet lesson, they even spent all of their free time together.

She felt, at this point in time, she needed to make a decision:

a) should I stand up to my feelings for Dr. Brewer and leave Jack? or

b) should I wiggle some freedom from home with some hobby or other in order to be able to meet him outside of surgery times?

c) did not dawn on her.

She tried to think of some way she could leave the house without arousing suspicion.

She couldn't play an instrument, and if she decided on a subscription to concerts, Jack would naturally also subscribe and go with her.

Plenty to do in their garden, was there scope for an outlet there? Not really. If she decided to register for a course on gardening, Jack would definitely think it a grand idea and would register, as well.

What interest would Jack not share with her?

The answer was so simple, she couldn't think why she hadn't thought of it straight away. Cookery!

She checked the internet for suggestions. Oh my God, this was going to take ages. However, through a simple system of logical reduction, she managed to get the list down to three. On further checking and a new criteria – she needed to be able to put her newfound cookery knowledge on the table at home without actually having had to learn anything – she was done.

She registered for a basic cookery course starting the following Wednesday; six weeks on minced meat. Seems unpretentious enough, she could handle that. And, it would mean one evening at the Community Centre to check out 'the scene', and the other five evenings, she could skip the course and spend them with Eamon Brewer. That would give her ample time to decide on her next step.

She was extremely pleased with herself, and when Wednesday finally arrived, she turned up five minutes early for the class. She wasn't, however, the first one there. A young man was sitting in the corner. She recognized him immediately; he was the man who sometimes picked up the prescriptions for the hospice - Connor? Yes, that was his name: Connor

Connor

Who is Connor?

"YES!" he shouted, not that anyone could hear him, but it felt good to be getting somewhere. The Matron at the Hospice hadn't seemed to like him when he started working there. He was sure of that. She had put all kinds of stones in his path and given him the worst of shifts with the most awkward colleagues

She had definitely known what she was doing. It wasn't that she was testing him. She wanted him to give up. She could see the writing on the wall; he had always yielded when things got tough. But he had knuckled down and proven her wrong. He had worked really hard to prove to everyone, including himself, that he could, if he wanted to.

They obviously now really did appreciate what he was doing.

No Sunday shift had been too much to ask of him, no night shift that he had refused, and there was not a person he had cared for that hadn't wished to have met him earlier in life. He spread optimism and positivity where none would normally be found.

He was so grateful.

He had hated, absolutely loathed school. Detested the institution, the teachers, and most of all, the discipline that had been expected of him. Resented the expectations that had been set in him. He had begun to dislike himself for even contemplating complying. So, he stopped.

Playing truant had been easy enough – he just stopped going to school. Unfortunately, it had only taken two weeks for the school to react. Fortunately, it had taken a lot longer for any authority to react in any effective way. This had given him the time to hit the streets. Life was not without complications on the streets. One of them was that almost everyone knew him. He was a local lad and everyone knew who his parents were. So, he was forced to move on to a town where he wasn't known. There was, however, a disadvantage here: he didn't know his way around. Bottom line was he dropped out of school, and dropped out of his family.

He had deemed life complicated, and after "the move," it gained in complexity. The street scene was tough, and he was vulnerable. Life became darn right hard. He found he could trust no-one. He did odd jobs to earn a little cash (indeed some very "odd" jobs), and he mostly slept at the shelter for homeless (they took particular pity on him due to his age, even though he looked a couple of years older than he really was). He smoked a lot, though mainly cigarettes. Surprisingly enough, he engaged in very little drug-taking. He tried a little, when he was persuaded to, but was never really hooked. This fact alone was to be his greatest advantage later.

One day, as he was walking the rounds in the park, a middle-aged man drew him into a conversation which was to turn his life around. It had started so simply, more like small talk than anything else, but had quickly proceeded to become an intimate exchange of past lives, views, and expectations. He hadn't realized that he was still capable of aspiring to anything. The next day he had gone back to the park, at the same time, in the hope of meeting with the man again. Finn was there - waiting for him.

He hadn't realized how much he had missed intimate conversations. In fact, conversations of any kind. He hadn't even registered just how much he despised his "new" life. Finn made him see it and made him face up to it. He also convinced him that he had to do something about it. Finn had a seasoned eye for those who could still be rescued; he was a social worker and his heart was in the job.

Finn led him back to the real world.

It had been a struggle, but he had persevered. He had refused to go back to his parents, a stance which prompted disbelief at the home, but they had seen how seriously he took the therapy lessons and helped him through the tribulations. He now knew that his intense animosity towards school was merely a proxy hostility, which had provoked his journey away from his oh, so middle-class life and his oh, so middle-class parents.

If only he had talked to them, he would never have needed to talk to Finn.

For him interpersonal communication was now ultimately important. It had given him a new sense of being, a unique feeling of worth, of value. A revived life.

He thought he had been rock bottom, but he had been nowhere near it. Finn, his saviour, had arrived on the scene in good time - he had been so lucky.

When he had applied for a job at the hospice, he didn't really have much hope of being offered anything. Little did he know how much Finn was doing in the background. He was overjoyed when he was accepted for a trial period, during which he was to do a training course. He felt like he had been thrown in the deep end once he started to work, though. The Matron watched every move he made. She left no stone unturned when it came to making him look irresponsible, or incompetent. She eyed him with more than a little suspicion when he sat by the bedside of the patients much longer than normally expected and held hands, and talked, or listened, depending on the person. She had done all she could to put him off staying. He was sure that she even checked his room when he was on shift, just to see if she could find something compromising. She couldn't.

She wasn't a matron at all, really. She was the manager of the hospice. Everyone just

called her "Matron," not only behind her back, either. He had always found this slightly peculiar. Maybe it was due to the fullness of her body, which matched her voluminous voice, or maybe due to the fact that she had previously been a senior nurse of some authority in a high-profile specialist clinic in London. Whatever the reason, it was a given.

One day, by pure coincidence, they had been alone in the staff lounge and he had asked her if it bothered her being called Matron. She said at first it had, just a little, but now she was more than used to it, and now she felt quite at home with it. As she left, she had thanked him for asking.

When she had called him into her office, he had been sure it was not good news. She made him sit in that horrible low chair in front of that huge desk, and she throned on her chair behind it. Then she began: how long he had been there, how many people he had helped through their last phases, how much extra responsibility he had taken on, how much his colleagues relied on his judgement, and how much she appreciated his work. Then she had paused. He had waited. The pause seemed endless.

Then she had said that the executive committee of the charity which owned the hospice would be meeting the next day.

Here it comes, this is the end, he thought.

She was going to recommend him for the position of resident carer. It wasn`t her decision, of course. The executive committee would decide – the following day. Then they would inform him of their decision by email.

Should he get the position, he would have to move out of his room and into the flat in the annex.

Just like that, she had said it. Then she had wished him a good evening and he had left her office.

And then, he saw it, in black and white, on the screen in front of him; the position was officially his.

He was struck by an intense emotion, a feeling of success. The flat was a two-bedroom flat, with a balcony, large bathroom and fully-fitted kitchen. A far cry from his room with en-suite bathroom and small kitchen block in the corner, which he presently had and which he had considered near to paradise when he first arrived.

A flat to which he could invite visitors – such luxury he had not expected so soon.

It was definitely time to embark on the next stage of his journey – re-engaging with his parents. He hadn`t seen them, had had no contact with them for over five years now. It was going to be difficult, but he felt well-prepared.

A further advantage of the "senior" position would be that he could now define which days he was free. He could even go so far as to have the same day every week. He could then also embark on a further stage of his self-revival; he could maybe do a course.

Nothing too academic, he didn`t want to go that far. Maybe something practical; he checked what was still on offer in the way of evening classes. Most of them had already started, or were already full, or were completely out of the question. One article caught his eye: the Community Centre was offering a basic cookery class – six weeks; topic minced meat.

Ticked all his boxes, so he submitted a registration. Bingo, he was in. The following Wednesday evening off, he strolled to town with a skip in his stride. He was just so lucky. He was also fifteen minutes early. He arrived together with the teacher – Rachel.

Rachel

Why is Rachel running this course?

"What am I letting myself in for now?" she asked herself for the dozenth time in the last hour. She could be quite satisfied with her life, for life had been good to her in many aspects. She had chosen to become a teacher, and she had achieved it. She had chosen to teach history, focus; political history, and she had. Thus, she was in the enviable position to be doing exactly what she wanted. Unfortunately, things change during one's lifetime – things that one does not necessarily have any influence on whatsoever. She was sure that it wasn't her that had changed, it was the pupils. Or, more precisely, their interpretation of what she was teaching them. They no longer saw any need for the knowledge she had to offer. They were all somehow preoccupied.

Her husband had died three years ago – suddenly, from one day to the next. Heart attack in the garden. Gone.

Her two children were both away at university. One in the middle of her BSc degree, the other just starting his PhD.

She had no-one to look after, or to cook for, or even to talk to. She was lonely.

She needed to change something.

This is no easy task for someone so close to retiring age. Especially someone who, hand on heart, didn't really want to change anyway. It would have to be something affiliated to what she has been doing all her life. Just a tweak more than a real change.

It was Edmond who would help her out of this dilemma. They had chatted after the last local residents' meeting. He was responsible for the local Community Centre and was looking for new ways of getting a more varied, diverse approach to community centre life. He thought too many people had the idea that Community Centres were just Youth Clubs with another name. He had already convinced the town council that a complete rethink should take place. He would love to offer classes to adults. He was sure he had struck a good idea, at least a good start. All permissions and grants were in place.

He wanted to offer cookery classes. They had an industrial kitchen – not a school kitchen, but one that would suffice. He had also been successful in convincing some local retailers to sponsor the foodstuffs needed for the courses. All he needed now was someone to run the course. A domestic science teacher (or rather, a home economics teacher) would probably not be interested, as the idea would not be serious enough on the cooking side – then it struck him: a history teacher whose hobby was cooking!

Would she consider it?

Indeed, she would. She thought it would be a challenge, but one which she felt she actually wanted. She could get to know the participants and then pick dishes to suit them. Yes, quite fun – just what she needed.

For the first evening, she thought she would take something that would tick a number of boxes for a number of people. She had absolutely no idea who had signed up, so filling, nutritious, and tasty. She decided on one of her family's favourites: Cheesy Ratatouille, always went down well with them and she was pretty sure whoever had signed up probably didn't know the recipe already.

She was unexpectedly uneasy as she entered the kitchen at the Community Centre for her first evening. Although, maybe excited would be a better word – she was certainly looking forward to facing a room of participants who actually wanted to be there.

The time came to get started and she faced Janice (absorbed in her own misery), Lavinia (pondering her position at home), Andrew (purely inattentive), Tina (wrapped up in her own little world), Heather (distracted by the plans forming in her head), and Connor – just glad to be there.

She didn't notice the preoccupation; she was just happy to be teaching something slightly different, but something she loved to do, and was pleased to have some students who actually wanted to learn from her.

All the ingredients had all been donated. They could cook to their hearts' desire and then eat together at the end of each evening.

She explained to everyone that she hadn't fixed the exact recipes they would cook (she missed the look on Heather's face), they could all have a say in that (she misunderstood the look on Andrew's face). When they sat down at the end of the evening, they could give a little information about themselves (she misinterpreted the look on Janice's face) and why they were here (she misjudged the look on Lavinia's face), and she could plan things from there (she couldn't assess the look on Tina's face).

So much more enjoyable than a strict curriculum to be followed whatever happens – she looked Connor in the eye and saw his smile

Cheesy Ratatouille

So, minced meat.

She explained a few basics but soon realized that no-one was particularly interested in this, so she decided to march onwards. She was going to be using beef mince throughout, to ensure that no-one took offence.

Today, each team of two would have:

400gr. beef mince, one aubergine, one onion, one garlic clove, one courgette, one red pepper, one yellow pepper, one tin of chopped tomatoes (delivered by the sponsor in place of fresh) 200gr. grated cheese, salt, pepper and some "herbs de Provence," and some cooking oil. They would conjure up:

"Cheesy Ratatouille with mince."

Three teams then. She looked at the group, they were not making any signs of grouping themselves. Janice stood next to Lavinia but didn`t really seem at ease there. Connor was standing next to Heather but that didn`t look too promising, either. Andrew even seemed to be shifting away from Tina. It was Connor who spoke, "Let`s put our names in a bowl and draw teams," he suggested. The group looked relieved.

The result of the draw was:

Team One: Heather & Janice

Team Two: Tina & Connor

Team Three: Andrew & Lavinia

Each team was handed the vegetables and told to dice the aubergine and onion, and cut the peppers into thin slices. Rachel was very surprised to note how difficult this exercise proved to be. She actually had to show Connor and Tina how to shell a pepper before cutting it (Andrew was helped by his teammate).

With the vegetables in the pan and everything well-stirred, and covered, they had 15 minutes to tide over – plenty of time to tidy up and turn the oven on – 175 degrees.

Rachel thought it rather peculiar that the group should be so placid. How come they weren't all chatting away? She decided it must be purely due to the fact that it was the first evening. Besides, there was more work to be done.

After adding the beef mince to the vegetables, they returned the pan to the hotplate for 5 minutes.

Then everything was put into an oven dish and covered with the grated cheese. 20 minutes later it, would be cooked and ready to eat.

During this time, they set the table. It seemed almost a given that the team members would sit next to each other. Rachel placed some fresh baguettes on the table and hoped that the food would do the trick and help them all finally relax.

They all sat down and the stage that Heather had been fearing most came. Rachel asked everyone to give a little background information about themselves so that she could better assess which meals would be best suited. With six participants and six evenings, they could choose one each.

* *Connor was eager to communicate his wish: he hadn't had any contact with his parents for around five years. Now, at least once settled in his new flat, he wanted to invite them over for a meal. Nothing extravagant. Something relatively normal, but easy to cook and, well, it should be slightly "different."

* *Tina suddenly realized that this was her wish, too. She lived with her parents, but the wish was indeed similar. It was her birthday in a couple of weeks. For the last seven years, she had invited her parents out for a meal to celebrate. This year would be different. She would cook a meal for her parents. Something out-of-the-ordinary. Something her mother wouldn't think of cooking.

Naturally, something she couldn't mess up, so not too difficult to cook.

*Andrew felt encouraged: he too, wanted to entertain at home. He didn't have the money to take any prospective girlfriends out for a meal, so he wanted something that was easy to cook but made a good impression – as if he was a crack at cooking – and something that didn't cost too much.

* Lavinia explained that for her, it was most important for something filling to be put on the table. With two hungry children to feed every evening, she was glad of any suggestions. Simple, filling, down-to-earth, good cooking. That was it.

* Janice now wished she had perked up earlier. She didn't want to give too much away. She decided to stick to absolute basics. She was a single mother, son aged eight. Left home in the morning with him and returned around the same time as him in the afternoon. Needed ideas for wholesome meals that could be cooked simply and quickly. Yes, that was enough info.

* Heather looked around – right here we go. She too, had one child. A daughter aged six. She too, worked every day. Left home around ten and arrived home earliest five in the afternoon - often later. Her husband, however, was home every day from 4.00 pm onwards, and he quite enjoyed cooking the evening meal. So, for her really, just something she could offer every now and again when the opportunity arose. No big deal.

The 20 minutes were up. The few minutes needed for the dish to cool down slightly seemed an awful long time.

Tina plucked up courage and said to Connor:

"I thought it would be more difficult."

"What exactly?"

"Well, cooking."

"We have only cooked one dish."

"Yes, but it wasn`t difficult, was it?"

"Maybe that was part of the plan – to lull us into a sense of false security."

"Oh, I see."

"You aren`t laughing, not even smiling."

"Why would I smile or laugh? Didn`t you mean what you said?"

"No, I didn`t. I was joking."

"Oh."

Connor was at a loss to understand how such a young woman could be so lacking in humour. It had been the same while they were cooking. She had been so serious and had done exactly what she had been told. By Rachel, or by him. She didn`t seem capable of deciding anything for herself and took everything at face value. No questions asked.

Connor was drawn into a conversation to his left with Janice:

"Well, that wasn`t so bad, was it?"

"Did you think it would be bad?"

"No, I`m saying it wasn`t bad. It was good."

"But you said, *so* bad."

"Did I?"

"Yes."

"Oh."

Connor noticed the negativity, he recognized it. Everything she said, she turned into a negative, even if she didn`t mean to. Every sentence she offered was laden with her sense of lacking something. Moreover, it seemed she didn't even realize she was doing it. How unfortunate, for herself and for all those around her. He found her hard to take.

Heather kept a very low profile – she really didn't want to get involved. After all, she wouldn't be here next week.

Andrew and Lavinia, on the opposite side of the table:

"Do you have any brothers and sisters?"

"Yes, I have a sister, but she lives in France."

"So you holiday in France, then, do you?"

"No. I haven't seen her since she went over there."

"Sorry to hear that."

"You needn't be. We never got on very well, even as kids."

"Ah, yes. Sibling rivalry can be intense."

"It wasn't that. She was a big crack in athletics and I hated sports of any kind. Except maybe swimming, and diving."

"Oh."

Andrew couldn't understand why she kept doing that. She always assumed something and followed it up. It had been the same while they were cooking. He was certain the only reason she had peeled and cut the onion was because she had assumed he didn't want to. She had really suffered for it. The tears just ran down her cheeks. Maybe he was wrong, but there was something of a martyr about this woman.

The food arrived and conversation lulled, intermittent phrases on the weather, local events, and the general state of the high street pavement. Thank goodness, thought Rachel – at least good old-fashioned small talk is not uncommon to them.

They all agreed the meal tasted more than just good. It was so filling that they couldn't finish all of it. In fact there was a whole dish left.

Rachel suggested Janice take it home with her. She could heat it up for her and her son tomorrow evening. Everyone agreed this was a splendid idea. Janice was thrilled at the idea as it meant one less thing to have to worry about tomorrow.

Heather became rather restless. She just wanted to be out of here. She was longing for some kind of bell to ring to announce "end of lesson." Rachel had other ideas though,

the kitchen needed to be cleaned first. She then let them all go with the proclamation that next week`s dish would be 'Meat Roll with Goat`s Cheese Filling.' As this could be prepared in advance and stored for cooking later, it was perfect for Heather.

"Damn!" thought Heather.

Rachel's Realm

Rachel arrived home around 10.30 pm; it had been quite an exhausting evening, but then, that was probably quite normal. It had been something out of the ordinary for her - teaching her first evening class, and her first cookery class. She couldn't just go to bed. She had to dwell a little on how the evening had progressed. She had hoped it would be different from her regular classroom work, and it was. Working with adults was different, for a start. Watching adults interact and listening to their conversations (she hadn't set out to do that, but it was impossible not to) was quite impelling.

She had arrived at the same time as the first participant and was quite surprised; so young and so eager. Then he had just sat down and waited for the others to arrive. Hadn't spoken to her, just let her get on with sorting the food. Maybe he didn't have such fond memories of his former teachers.

The next to arrive had been no better. She had just looked around and then approached the lad, Connor. They obviously hadn't any inclination to speak to each other. It was quite a surreal situation, almost as if they were pretending not to know each other.

Even funnier, however, was the young lady whose silhouette could be seen outside the door. She stood there for a good few minutes before finally deciding to enter. She was certainly a reluctant student. She had thrown a semi-smile to the other woman.

The next two were women, chatting but not intently, not as if they really wanted to, just as if they felt obliged. They were not at ease with each other, that much was certain.

And then the second young man, who, on arrival had glanced quickly in the direction of two in the corner (subdued a sign of recognition) but decided against anything more than a (very) casual Hi!

Rachel had thought she was being held for a fool – is this Candid camera, or what?

It was almost as if they were all playing a role, trying to fool her (or each other?) into believing something that was not true. She could literally feel this whole scenario wasn't right. Bringing sustainable group dynamics to this group was not going to be easy.

As she drank her cup of tea, Rachel felt quite proud. Although, admittedly, it was not all her doing, the evening had turned out well.

Connor, the eager one, had turned out to be a God-send. It was he who had suggested drawing names for the teams and had set the stage for a pleasant environment. The dynamics had already changed after the cooking was finished. Although only general in nature, and not particularly open, the conversations were relaxed and casual.

The few snippets of personal information that she had received from each of them would help her put together the right recipes.

Heather had remained almost secretive all evening, but maybe she would ease up a little when her recipe was cooked next week. The decision to make Meat Roll had been quite spontaneous, but even on reflection, it seemed to be the right one. It was a continental touch to family eating, so just what she had asked for – something slightly

different when it was her turn to do the cooking, and no big deal when it came to preparation.

For the week after, she was still dithering a little but had almost decided on Cottage Pie. That would be good for Lavinia's family. Growing children need something really filling, and this was THE perfect family meal.

Side Dishes

A week can go by so fast; Wednesday had arrived, and the participants headed off once again to the Community Centre, leaving behind what complemented their lives – their side dishes, so to speak.

Their reactions to the course had been varied:

*Tina`s parents were pleased she was doing the course. They saw it as a step in the right direction and were thrilled at the added advantage of having the house to themselves for the evening. Not that Tina was a burden, or a hindrance to their social life, but somehow they had got into routines that hardly included socializing with their friends during the week. They had invited Ted and Jean over for a round of cards.

*Heather`s husband was very pleased she had signed up for the course. It had made his decision so much easier. Just how long had he been yearning to do the "creative writing" course at night school? He just hadn`t managed to pluck up – what? Courage, maybe – no, simply the will to effectively register for it. Now, with Heather doing her cookery course, he had no qualms whatsoever.

*Lavinia`s family were, however, in no way happy when she had announced her decision to do a cookery course every Wednesday. Wednesday was, as far as they were concerned, simply the worst possible day for her to be out of the matrix: George had cricket training, Chelsey had choir practice, and Ian had his tennis session. Now she had an appointment as well. How was that supposed to work? The children considered it extremely selfish as it meant they had to either cycle, or hitch lifts with friends` parents who didn`t feel the need to go on a self-searching mission. Ian wasn`t too bothered either way, although he would have preferred her to be "on call." What if he needed her to pick him up because he couldn`t drive home himself due to injury? That had already happened on a number of occasions.

*As for Tim, he had found it surprising, in fact almost an insult, that Janice had started a cookery course almost immediately after he had left. Was that what he was good for? Keeping them all well-fed? Is that what she now missed? The good food! Dylan certainly was of the opinion that it was a good idea – he really didn't think much of his mother's cooking skills. Not much else had changed for Tim, though. Janice still had those same negative inclinations that she, truth be known, always had had. The very ones which he now found so terribly annoying. He just couldn't take it any longer. Either she had to change, or he had to change something.

*Andrew's neighbours hadn't even noticed the change in his routine as he left for the second Wednesday evening in a row, purely because he hadn't had a noticeable routine in the first place.

*Connor's colleagues were puzzled. They had been thrilled when they heard of his promotion as they honestly felt he had deserved it. They had, however, underestimated the consequences it would have on them. He now had a completely different schedule, how come he had to have every Wednesday evening off? He had never refused to change shifts before.

Meat Roll with Goat`s Cheese Filling

Rachel had been quite satisfied with the way things had gone the week before. At first, when she had seen her group she was very worried that they would in no way mingle. She had been proven wrong.

Tina spotted Connor already seated at the counter where they had been the week before.

"I suppose we`re a team again," she said

"Only if you want to," Connor replied. He tried his understanding smile on her. It worked in most cases. She smiled back. It had worked. She thought they made a good team as they were the only obvious beginners in the group. He thought they should stay together for another week to see if he could break the facade which she carried around so prominently with her.

As Lavinia entered the room, Andrew looked up and smiled at her. She smiled back, and assumed that the teams were obviously going to be the same as last week, so she crossed the room to take her place next to him. He assumed she had assumed this but did nothing to deter her. He thought it might actually be fun to prod her into doing what SHE wanted, rather than what she thought he wanted. He was ready to give it a go.

Janice was running late. She had forgotten the dish and had had to go back home and fetch it. Good job she had, though. As she walked into the kitchen, she noticed Dylan`s sports bag. How come she had not noticed it before? He would need it for school. As he was staying at his father`s again, she felt compelled to deliver it to Tim`s parents` house. Fortunately, they weren`t in. Only Tim and Dylan were there.

"You`re living with your parents after all then?"

"What do you mean by 'after all'?"

It wasn't a good start; she could tell that immediately. His back stiffened, his eyes tightened and he lifted his chin just slightly. She couldn't be bothered, so she let it go. Handed over the sports bag, gave Dylan a quick kiss on the cheek (which he just as quickly brushed off) and left them standing on the porch.

Even though she was late, she wasn't the last to arrive.

Heather wasn't anywhere to be seen yet. So, unfortunately, Janice was seemingly without a teammate since the teams were, quite obviously, like they had been the previous week.

Rachel decided it would be better to get started, even though it was effectively "Heather's" recipe, and she was still missing. "Meat Roll with Goat's cheese Filling and Zaziki," she declared. She explained that this could be served with rice, or even chips, but today, they would be eating fresh baguettes with their meal as the local bakery had, yet again, been so generous as to donate.

Each team had 400 gr beef mince, one egg, breadcrumbs and a 140gr pack of goat's cheese, plus the obligatory salt, pepper, basil, and oregano.

They placed the mince in a bowl and seasoned it well. Then cracked the egg into the bowl and mixed the ingredients with a spoon.

The door opened, and Heather walked in – slightly flustered.

She had actually been outside the door for a while, still considering whether she really did want to enter. She did. So, in she strode. She had ummed and aahed, before leaving home. The original idea was to have time for Eamon, but somehow, the parameters had suddenly changed. Jack had now started a "creative writing" course, which took place every Thursday. He had said, "I hope it will be okay." Of course it would be, it left her Thursday evenings open. She could stay with Eamon tomorrow.

She apologised, to Rachel, to the group, and to Janice.

The stodgy mix in the bowl didn't look very appetizing, but it was early in the evening. In order to make the mixture more solid and easier to form, they added some breadcrumbs.

The goat's cheese is crumbly stuff. It proved rather difficult to cut it properly.

Rachel checked all three rolls once they were complete - it was especially important that the roll was properly sealed, or the cheese might ooze out during cooking. They had thirty minutes to wait for the result.

As this was a somewhat adapted version of a Greek meatloaf, Rachel had decided that zaziki would go well.

So, each team peeled and cut their cucumber and mixed the pieces into 150gr of Greek joghurt. A few drops of olive oil, a little garlic and some salt and pepper completed the zaziki, and they could set the table.

"Have you ever been to Greece?" asked Connor of his teammate

"No, I've never really been on a proper summer holiday since I left school."

"Good heavens, why on earth not?"

"Never got around to it, I suppose. Every time I thought I might, one of my parents got sick, or – one time, my brother announced he was getting married. So, I never booked."

"Oh, yes, you said that you live with your parents. Are they in ill-health?"

"No, not at all. They are as healthy as anyone."

"So, you could go on holiday whenever you like, then."

"Well, yes."

On the next table, Andrew addressed his teammate:

"It looked like you had done that before. You`re not really a beginner, are you?" "Well, no. I have a family to feed, remember."

"It is OK. I just happened to notice your prowess."

"Sorry, I thought you wanted me to help you. I shouldn`t have, should I? You need to learn."

"Hey, it`s fine, really. I can learn a lot by watching you."

"You should just tell me if I start to play "mother" with you. My husband says I do it all the time."

"We could agree to share. Or, we could agree to ask each other."

"Well, yes."

"I suppose you`d like to sit here again?" said Janice to her teammate

"Well, we sat here last week, and it was OK, but if you want to sit somewhere else…"

"No, no, it was fine. I was just asking."

"I thought maybe you wanted to swap places or something."

"Why would you think that?"

"Well, because you said 'I suppose' at the beginning of your sentence."

"That was enough for you to think I wanted to sit somewhere else?"

"Well, yes."

The thirty minutes were up. The meat rolls looked ready, and tasted delicious.

They sat together and ate together.

Suddenly, Connor said, "Tina is thinking of going to Greece on holiday now."

A look of astonishment filled her face, but the reaction of the group was such that she played along. They all thought it would be a grand idea. Had anyone already been there? Janice, Lavinia and Heather all had experiences to share. What was it like? Where were the best hotels? Should one really trust the internet for information? Was it not better to go to the travel agents and let them arrange everything? What about travel insurance? What about health insurance? Could one go there to work (this was Andrew)

Time flew by.

By the end of the evening, Tina was as good as convinced that she may actually really make it to Greece for her next summer holiday.

They cleared up the kitchen and were sent on their way with the information that next week`s recipe would be a down-to-earth one: good old Cottage Pie.

Excellent for Lavinia, very good for Janice and Heather, but equally good for everyone else.

There was one meat roll still left. Who would like to take it home? They all looked at each other.

Janice said that Dylan had loved the cheesy ratatouille last week – however, they all agreed that Heather should take the meat roll home. After all, it was *her* recipe.

Rachel's Realm

As Rachel sat herself down in the armchair in her living room, she sipped at her tea and pondered over the evening she had just experienced.

It was indeed different to a school classroom. Although children, and adolescents, were interesting to watch in their interaction, grown adults actually gave so much more away. It was quite fascinating.

The teams from the week before had remained in place and the people had seemed much more at ease with each other. That in itself was no great wonder, but the fact that they were such different characters, and yet somehow so strangely close after such a short time.

The two beginners obviously felt better being together and Connor was obviously an easy-going chap. He led Tina by the hand almost, so funny that she should need that, being the older of the two.

Lavinia was not so easy-going, why on earth was she in the course? She was pleasant enough, and helped Andrew where she felt he needed it. He, though, seemingly wanted to be asked if he wanted help. It was purely down to his openness, that all was turning out well. She had heard him say to Lavinia that they should agree to ask, before deciding what to do.

The two ladies were quite a pair. One later than the other – she had almost thought Heather wasn't going to turn up at all, even though she had purposely defined the recipe as hers. Somehow, they didn't seem to be getting on as well as the others.

She had been quite surprised to see how Connor had become such a pivotal element in the group. He seemed to be able to sense when someone needed a prod in the right direction. Tina had really brightened up when he told everyone about her plans to go to Greece. Almost as if she wouldn't have even mentioned it if he hadn't said anything.

The change in the young woman was quite remarkable – and it certainly made for lively conversation.

Connor was such a likeable lad, but there was something almost mysterious about him. He was so communicative, and he yet held back when it came to himself. He was honest and yet seemed to be somehow secretive.

Should she do his recipe next? Oh, no – she suddenly remembered -Tina`s birthday. She needed to get Tina`s recipe in soon – why hadn`t she thought about that before? Too late now. Next week was Cottage Pie, but the week after would hopefully still suffice. Something slightly different, that the mother would not expect and would probably not cook herself. That`s it - Stuffed Green Peppers with Rice.

Side Dishes

Another week on, other side dishes were being served:

Eamon was in conflict with his conscience. He really liked Heather, more than that – he could have imagined sharing his life with her if the circumstances were different. Of course, he had known from the start that she was married. He couldn't pretend he didn't. He had meant well; he wanted her to stay at the surgery, she was such a talented organizer. Maybe they should not have drunk that champagne. Somehow, they had rushed into something which he thought, in retrospect, was going to do more harm than good.

At Lavinia's place of work, her colleagues were riled. They were angry with her that she hadn't taken the job offer and they made it quite clear to her. In fact, they were doing everything they could think of to make her life difficult. If she had taken the job, as indeed everyone had expected her to do, they wouldn't now be lumbered with this awful pedantic chap who had been appointed instead of her. He had come directly from headquarters and was supposed to be a rising star in the company. At present, he was more of a pain and was testing the nerves of all and sunder.

Andrew's neighbours had finally noticed a difference - when he brought his last girlfriend home, they had cooked. That was novel. Hadn't changed the fact that she hadn't stayed for long, though. In fact, they hadn't seen her since. They couldn't quite comprehend him. He was definitely more pleasant than the previous chap in the flat, but somehow, he didn't have a steady routine in his life, which one should maybe expect in a young person starting out in his career. He was easy-going enough, but not open. Was he as honest as they thought?

Unfortunately for Tim, he found he was no further in his plan for the future. Things were not going as he had thought. He had imagined that Janice would ask him why, demand to know why, he had left them both. She had brushed on the question on the Sunday he left, but since then, she seemed just resigned to the fact that he was gone. She didn't even see how Dylan was suffering. How come he had not noticed what kind of a person he had been living with? He really loved her, more than he wished to admit, but she had this unfortunate way of articulating herself. It always came across as negative. He thought he had known what she really meant, and it hadn`t unduly bothered him. But now, looking back, he had to ask himself, did he really always know what she meant, or did he just interpret it to fit what he desired?

Cottage Pie

Of course, Connor arrived first. Rachel greeted him with a smile, showing sincere warmth.

Janice had made a special effort to be punctual. She didn't want a repeat of last week's entry. She wanted to be there when the teams were allocated. She had a feeling that last week, she was somehow left with Heather because no-one else had wanted to team up with her. Not that she didn't like her, just that she'd prefer to team up with someone else this week.

She grabbed the opportunity and approached Connor.

"If you promise not to drop me into anything, I could be your teammate this week."

"Drop you into something? What on earth do you mean?"

"Poor old Tina. Didn't you see the look on her face when you said she was thinking of going to Greece?"

"She knew I meant well."

"I'm not sure she did. She looked more shocked to me."

"She sure played along well afterwards, though."

"She was probably trying to impress you."

"Listen, don't go down that road. If you want to feel negative about things, be my guest. But leave me out of it."

"Why should I feel negative about something which you did?"

"Because that is what you do."

"If necessary, I can find a lot of positive things around."

"Yes, if necessary, you can. You just don't often see the necessity."

"I can see them if they are there."

"I have patients in the hospice who are more positive than you are."

"You work in a hospice?"

"Yes. They have every reason to be negative. They are literally waiting for the pearly gates to open up."

"You can't compare me to people on death row."

"I wouldn't even compare my patients to people on death row. On death row, you know why you are there. Most of my patients do not. They have to come to terms with the fact that fate has put them there."

"I didn't mean …"

"Yes, you did. I'm sorry to have to say this, but people like you make me very angry."

"You think I am a negative person. Full stop."

"I do. You prefer to see the negative side of things. You go looking for it with a toothcomb, if necessary."

"Sorry, you've lost me."

Heather had also made a special effort not to be late. She didn't fancy apologizing again. She'd had enough of apologies for one day anyway. Not that it had been her apologizing this afternoon. Eamon had apologized profusely, overdid it, really. He had an appointment he couldn't alter. They wouldn't be able to see each other this evening as planned. When he offered tomorrow, she had accepted both his apology and the change of plan. She did find it rather odd that he had reacted the way he did to her willingness to meet up tomorrow. Almost as if he had expected her to say she couldn't possibly stay even later on a Thursday.

As she approached the door, she saw Andrew coming from the men's toilets. They greeted each other and entered the room together.

Janice and Connor were sitting together in what seemed like a serious conversation, so they sat down together.

"Do you come straight here from work?"

"No, I have to nip home to check on Emily, my daughter, first. What about you?"

"No, I didn`t get a shift today. I was in town."

"Well, aren`t you the lucky one? Having a day off in the middle of the week. I wish I could have that."

"I wish I didn`t have to, actually. I would prefer to work."

"I`m sorry to hear that. Have you managed to find a girlfriend to taste your wares, yet?"

"Actually, I did try out the ratatouille. A girl I met at the pub last week came on Friday, and we cooked it together. It was fun. And it was tasty. I quite surprised myself."

"That`s great news."

"Er, well, no. I haven`t heard from her since. I`m afraid that episode is now just another one of my almost, but not quites."

"Sorry, I can`t follow."

Tina could hardly wait to tell everyone her news. At the weekend she had been to the travel agents` in town and had picked up some travel brochures on Greece. She had made up her mind – she was going to go to Polichrono for two weeks early next summer. She would book when she went into town again at the weekend. She was almost a little sad when she saw that the other four were already seated in what looked like teams. She sat down and waited for Lavinia, resigned to the fact that she would be her teammate for the day.

In came Lavinia, dead on time and with a face like death warmed up. Her mood didn`t improve when she realized Andrew had found himself a new teammate. He had obviously had enough of her already. She took her place next to Tina.

"Ready for your recipe, then?"

"What?"

"Your recipe. That`s what Rachel said last week – cottage pie. Perfect for you."

"Oh, right."

"Had a bad day, have you?"

"No worse than any other day I've had recently. Things are just not going my way."

"I`m sorry to hear that."

"Don`t worry yourself. I`ll pull through, I always have."

"You may be pleased to know I`m going to Polichrono."

"Sorry, I don`t get you."

Rachel was picking up some strange vibrations from the group this week. It was definitely time to get started with the cooking. Time to focus on what they were here for. There was a lot of preparation to be done this week. A lot of chopping to do.

First, there were the potatoes to peel.

While these were cooking, the other vegetables had to be prepared: an onion, two small carrots, and a celery stalk, all cut into small cubes.

Rachel did feel obliged to say that this part of the work could be simplified, and thus quickened up, if canned vegetables were used.

Judging the amount of beef stock to use was challenging – not too much, just enough so that the meat stays moist, and not too much or the pie will ooze moisture.

After all the ingredients were in the casserole dish on went the cheese topping.

Off into the pre-heated oven for just long enough for the cheese to melt.

As this can be eaten with merely a fork, the table was set within seconds.

They sat down together, in teams still, but somehow searching for conversation beyond those "team" boundaries. Maybe it was a good thing that the preparation had been more intense this week, they had all needed a little time to cool off and/or cool down.

Except Tina, who was still on a high and couldn't wait to tell everyone her news.

"I have news for you all – I'm going to Polichrono."

"Wow. That is great! Congratulations!"

"Why congratulations? She's going on holiday, for Christ's sake."

"Hey, this is important for Tina. She hasn't been on holiday since she was at school."

"I've been to Polichrono. It was super. Which hotel are you staying at?

"The Regal, I think it is."

"Hm. Don't know that one. We stayed at the Royal. Could it be that? It was just superb."

"Oh yes, you could be right, I'm not sure."

"Sounds quite posh. I bet it is expensive."

"No. It is part of a package deal. I thought it was quite reasonably priced – in comparison."

"I`m really pleased you`re doing this. Janice thought I had dropped you in it last week. She was worried about you."

"I almost tried to stop him. I did."

"Almost. I heard that word earlier. Andrew what do you say to all this? You`re very quiet all of a sudden."

"I can`t say much at all, really. I`m really pleased for Tina, but I`ve never been to Greece, so I can`t give her any advice there."

"Is that an almost, but not quite then?"

"No, it is simply a never done."

Rachel was so pleased that the atmosphere was now decidedly better. There's nothing like a good, tasty meal to clear the air - it always works.

This week, there was nothing left over, everything had been eaten up.

Tina had had such a good evening; never before had she been the centre of attention in a group. Never before had she felt so, so good. She felt even better when she heard that "her" recipe was to be next week. Rachel hadn`t forgotten that she wanted to cook it as her birthday dinner. So, even without knowing exactly when the birthday was, she had obviously calculated it must be in one, or two week`s time. Next week, they would cook Stuffed Green Peppers with Rice.

Rachel's Realm

Back at home, Rachel relaxed in her armchair. She decided it was a gin and tonic evening; it had been a rather bumpy start with the group, and it was such a relief that the evening had ended so amicably.

Janice had seemed quite pleased to have a new team partner, only to bulldoze poor Connor about his treatment of Tina last week. Funny, she hadn`t noticed that; it must have happened while she had her wits elsewhere. What really surprised her was how Connor had reacted. It seemed quite atypical, although how would she know what was typical for Connor - she hardly knew him. She certainly hadn`t expected him to be so brutal in his (verbal) attack on Janice. Of course, she too, had noticed how terribly negative the woman seemed, but she had thought it was maybe due to the fact that she was a single mother. That must be very trying at times. Or, maybe purely and simply a chip on her shoulder, there are such people around. It seemed not - she really was a negative person.

Just fancy Connor working at the hospice. She hadn`t really put too much thought into where he worked. Her thoughts on him were centered more around the fact that he had said he had no contact with his parents. How could something like that happen to such an amiable young man?

Heather was warming up nicely. She was obviously used to talking to people and winning over their trust. Poor Andrew, though. She felt sorry for him. He seemed a friendly enough chap and yet was so obviously not popular with the ladies in his immediate circle of friends. She began to feel slightly embarrassed at the thought of how much of the individual conversations she had overheard, but then the feeling blew over very quickly.

Tina, well Tina seemed almost a different person now. So transformed; she walked in, saw Connor chatting with Janice, and her face fell. She was not to be sidelined from her glee, though. She was so full of herself this evening that you could almost grasp her joy. Only to find herself teamed up with a Lavinia of the worse sort – what a nasty mood, she had. What had she said, "things never go my way," well, that would probably explain why she was in the group at all.

If she thought about it, she could be so pleased that Lavinia and Janice were not one team this evening – imagine that – Lavinia in a stinking mood and Janice determined to be negative, whatever came along.

Thank goodness for Tina – and Connor. Yet again, he had shown how open he is in conversation with others – yet still to open up about himself. What is it about him?

Maybe I should do his recipe next? No, she couldn't quite up her mind what to offer. But, for Andrew, she had an idea. Potato Lasagne with Mince wrapped in Bacon, would be perfect. Makes a very good impression but is not too complicated to prepare. At least, not as complicated as it looks at first glance

Side Dishes

What may essentially be of secondary importance, sometimes causes the most difficulties. Indeed, the week had not been easy in any of the scenarios.

Tina`s parents had suffered a shock, her father more than her mother. He had fallen off the ladder whilst working in the garden, and Tina had taken him to the hospital. Fortunately, nothing was broken but it did bring home to them the fact that they should be so grateful that Tina was so close by and could help them whenever they needed it.

Eamon had tried to initiate a shift in his relationship to Heather. He couldn`t do it. He obviously felt more for her than he wished to concede. In the end, he had just said he couldn`t make their date on Wednesday. He felt that would give him some extra time to assess his feelings and work out exactly how they should proceed. This may become very complicated.

Things had not gone well in Lavinia`s household, either. An important business partner of Ian`s was on a visit from Hong Kong and needed particular (time-intensive) attention. Chelsey`s choir had been chosen to represent the county in a high-profile event, and therefore she had to go to rehearsals every evening and all this at the same time as the county trials for the cricket team. No-one was in a mood to be particularly understanding when it came to having to take a (perceived) back seat in any matter.

Dylan was the first to notice a slight difference in his mother`s attitude. She seemed to be more thoughtful about what words she was using. When he had spoken to his father about it, Tim had just said it was wishful thinking. The week plodded on and got no better as far as he was concerned.

Andrew`s colleagues noticed a change for the worst in him. Although he had never been the most gregarious of creatures, he had at least been civil. Nowadays, he walked around like a bear with a sore head. Nothing seemed to cheer him up.

Even Connor`s environment was on a slant; "The Matron" at the hospice had spoken to him, somehow, she thought he wasn`t quite himself. He seemed so short-tempered and was not showing his usual relaxed self. What could be affecting him in such a way?

Stuffed Green Peppers with Rice

"I wanted to apologize before we go in," said Janice as she stood in front of Connor in the corridor.

"What for?" he said. He had been the first to arrive, as always, but for some reason, he was reluctant to enter the room this week. He hadn`t felt too good after what he had said to Janice last week. He had wanted to poke her into doing something about her attitude, but maybe he had gone just a little too far.

"Well, after our conversation last week, I thought an apology would be in order."

"You want to apologize for being you?"

"No, I want to apologize for sounding negative all the time."

"So, you do want to apologize for being you?" He couldn`t help himself.

"You`re being rather nasty."   Yes, he was.

"I told you, I am allergic to people like you, who only see things negatively when there is so much for them to be grateful for."

"How would you know what I should be grateful for?"

"Well, OK. So, tell me, what makes you see life in such a bad light?"

"My boyfriend has left me." Now it was out.

"Could be a good thing."

"No, it isn`t a good thing."

"And he`s definitely gone?"

"We have an eight-year-old son together. We lived together for nearly ten years. Then, one day, he upped and went."

"You had no idea?"

"No. I thought all was basically OK. We had a lovely house, both had steady jobs, good income and tried to give Dylan (our son) a stable life."

"<u>You said, basically</u> OK? And then, you <u>tried</u> to give him stability?"

"Yes, we tried hard to keep the family <u>safe.</u>"

"Safe? As in, keep danger away? So, you did think your family life was in danger?"

"No."

"You should listen to yourself."

"I find it hard talking about this."

"You haven`t mentioned the fact that you loved your boyfriend yet."

"Well, of course, I loved him."

"Did you tell him?"

"I didn`t need to."

"Did he tell you?"

"He didn`t need to."

"Why didn`t you get married?"

"He never asked me."

"Did you ask him?"

"How could I do that? We were happy with what we had, how things were."

"Obviously, he wasn`t."

"You certainly know how to make someone feel better."

"I want you to be better. You'll see, all this will help. Where do you live now?"

"In our house."

"He is OK with that?"

"Yes, he left me the house and a car."

"Where is he living now then?"

"With his parents. They have always hated me. Always thought I wasn't the right one for him."

"So, he doesn't have a new girlfriend, then. Don't you see what he is trying to do?"

"Hurt me, I guess. And he is being extremely successful."

"No, he's trying to send you a signal. A warning signal. You two really should talk."

They hadn't even noticed that everyone else had arrived in the meantime.

Everyone had walked right past the two of them, deep in conversation, standing so close to each other against the wall. Almost intimate, and yet not, merely intense.

Lavinia had been determined to be on time today. It wasn't easy to leave the house punctually. Somehow, everyone else's plans always seemed to be of a higher priority, and thus, her plans were difficult to push through. Today, however, she had managed to arrive at the same time as Tina. A stroke of luck, she thought as they walked into the room together. Only Rachel was there, so she manoeuvred their entrance so as to position themselves more-or-less in the corner. Slightly out of the way. She had something she wanted to say to Tina.

"I would like to apologize to you."

"For what?"

"Well. For my behaviour last week. It was out of order. I was in a bad mood, and you got the brunt of it."

"Apology accepted."

"Thank you. I feel a lot better now. Have you booked your holiday?"

"No, not yet. I am planning to go into town this weekend, and I`ll do it then. I had planned to go last Saturday, but my father fell off the ladder while working in the garden, and I had to go to the hospital with him."

"Is he OK?"

"Yes, he was very lucky. Just some very bad bruising and, of course, the shock."

"I suppose he`ll have to take it easy for a while then. Can your mum look after him?"

"Oh yes. She`s as fit as a fiddle. She can manage fine."

"You`re very lucky to have such independent parents. It must give you an immense ease of mind knowing they can do without you. Knowing you can live your life without worrying all the time."

"Well, yes. I suppose it does. I had never looked at it quite like that."

"Oh, you should. You should count yourself lucky. Not everyone is so free of responsibility, you know. Make use of the time while you can. That`s what I would say. Only too soon, you will have a family of your own, and then you have to take responsibility for them."

"Do you really think so?

"Why sure. YOLO. You only live once. I heard that saying a while ago, and I thought then, I wish someone had said that to me earlier in my life."

"Would you have done things differently, then?"

"Probably not. But I can claim that now, can`t I?"

"You have a family, don't you? That must be very satisfying."

"I think my family are very satisfied, yes."

Heather and Andrew were in deep conversation on the opposite side of the room. Heather was curious about what Andrew had meant last week.

"I'm sorry if this sounds too nosy, but I have been wondering what you meant last week about "almost, and not quites."

"It's a long story."

"Is that not what people say when they don't want to talk about something?"

"Maybe it is. But this really is a long story, as long as my life. You see, my life is one *big almost, but not quite*, from the beginning and right up to this very day."

"You don't strike me as a loser."

"Well, thank you. But I'm not saying I feel like a loser. I just feel like someone who isn't quite making it."

"Like getting halfway there and stopping rather than going that extra mile?"

"More like getting half-way there and being told – this is where you belong."

"You feel other people are determining your life?"

"Isn't that always the case?"

"It doesn't have to be. You're young – and independent. You have your life ahead of you. YOUR life, that could be, not the life others think you should have."

"You make it sound so easy. One needs to be given a break every now and again."

"One needs to take a break every now and again." (She felt this was a truly Freudian thing to say in her present situation, but didn't let on)

"Like grab what you can, and run?"

"No, more like grab what is rightfully yours."

"What I believe should be mine is not necessarily mine, though, is it?"

"Deep down, you will know if it is rightfully yours, and then you must fight for it, if necessary. Don't drop it like a hot potato just because the going gets a little tough."

"Are you saying you consider me a softie, then?"

"No. I'm saying you need to believe in yourself more. Define what you want to be, find it, nurture it, develop it, and treasure it."

Rachel had been waiting for what seemed the right moment to get started. She was somehow reluctant to break up the conversations as they were so in contrast to what

had been going on the week before. She had used the time to boil the water for the green peppers.

Her moment came as Janice and Connor finally entered the room.

Shelling the green peppers was something that the participants could remember from their first evening.

While the peppers were cooking in the water, the stuffing was prepared.

The stuffing itself was actually very easy, as long as they could remember how they had made the meat roll two weeks previously. They could.

Things were going so smoothly today.

The peppers needed to cool off a little, so the time was used to make the sauce. No lumps, and not too thin – the teams were getting really good.

Rachel had chosen rice to go with the meal, as this needed to be cooked for exactly the same length of time.

The participants set the table and were eager to know what this tasted like.

Really good – what did Rachel have in store for them next week? They wanted to know.

Well, with Andrew wishing to seduce the girls with his cooking skills, she was planning to try:

Potato Lasagne with Mince wrapped in Bacon

Andrew quickly became the centre of attention after this remark. Everyone wanted to know something about him. The fact that he lived on Kingsway was accepted, although Janice did wonder how he could afford it. Had he not said he didn't have much money? The fact that he had a degree led to some acknowledging nods, although Lavinia thought that was rather funny, considering he worked at the DIY store.

Then he even admitted to them all that he had tried out the cheesy ratatouille already on a girl he had met. She had thought it tasted great and was very impressed with his cooking, but didn't stay long enough to help clear up the kitchen.

Connor was eager to prove he could be a pleasant, friendly chap and chatted merrily. Commenting on this and that and making sure he didn't come close to the kind of screening Andrew was getting.

Once they found out that Andrew's sister now lived in France, there was no stopping the conversation. There was even more to be said about France than there had been about Greece.

By the end of the evening, there were no stuffed peppers left for anyone to take home with them.

What a successful evening.

Rachel's Realm

Well, what do you know? That was indeed an evening to remember. A little wine to celebrate, thought Rachel as she slumped into the armchair in the living room.

After the ups and downs of the previous week, everyone seemed to be intent on apologizing. - A sip of wine.

Lavinia seemed truly sorry for her mood last week, and to make up for it, she showed herself to be understanding and sincerely empathic. Listened to Tina intensely; and what a complicated person that Tina is. Can`t seem to make any kind of decision for herself at all. Probably never has done. But, was she really putting her parents first? She certainly made the impression that she is actually yearning to start a family of her own; or is she just yearning to move out and needs a reason/excuse? - Another sip of wine.

As Rachel sat there, Lavinia would not leave her thoughts. YOLO – she had spurted out. If only she had known the expression earlier in her life, she had said. Had she not also said, "My family is satisfied?" Oh, dear – maybe here is the reason for her presence in the course. - A further sip of wine.

Then there was Heather, giving Andrew almost motherly-type tips. Apologizing for something, couldn`t quite catch what for, unfortunately. Building his ego, cementing his belief in himself, telling him to grab the things he really wants in life. Quite forcefully, in fact. Maybe Heather was doing some self-help ritual, as well. It did seem as though she was cheerleading more than just Andrew - Yet another sip of wine.

Andrew indeed. He certainly opened up this evening. Poor chap, fancy going through university to be left out in the street when it comes to the job market. Seems it was not only the lady-friend side that needed some attention - The wine tasted good.

My goodness, thought Rachel, let`s not forget the best bit - Connor and Janice`s arrival. She was sure they had been outside the door for ages before they finally came in. There was a new quality of understanding between the two of them. Connor seemed at ease with her, and with himself. Janice seemed very pensive. - Final sip of wine.

Wasn`t it amazing to experience how people change in their interaction with each other? She hadn`t expected quite such a shift in the atmosphere and the, yes, the emotions, between the course participants. The steps being made were actually quite small, but they were making an impression that was almost unbelievable. The honesty which was developing and the openness of the statements was quite encouraging. She felt as if her feeling at the beginning of the course was only slightly wrong; they didn`t all know each other, but they all were, in some way, hiding something, or rather, had been hiding something.

After finally deciding the Mince Stew would be best for Connor`s parents, Rachel felt she could call it a day.

She went to bed, satisfied with her part in the happenings and almost dreading the early start the next day

Side Dishes

These can be varied at will. A little diversity never goes amiss.

Tina's colleagues had noticed a development which they couldn't quite pinpoint. It wasn't that she was more of a decision-maker than she used to be, but there was certainly a movement in her attitude towards change. She had even agreed to re-arrange the office furniture. Something which they had been talking about for some months but where discussions had always come to a halt when it came to Tina's desk. They weren't interested in where this change had come from. They just wanted to strike while the iron was hot.

Jack had also noticed something; he found that he and Heather, indeed all three of them were harmonizing so much better recently. Although they were all sometimes preoccupied with things outside of the family, they all seemed far closer now than at any time previously. He couldn't quite put his finger on it – when had this begun? How could such a transformation take place without active measures being taken? Can't possibly be only due to him and Heather each having a course to go to.

Lavinia's family, ever sensitive to change, was finally coming to terms with the fact that she no longer would accept always being the one to give in, or give up. It was strange, they thought, that they hadn't seen this coming. Even stranger that there didn't seem to be a particular event, or action which had spurned this adjustment.

Tim had eventually had to admit to himself, and to Dylan, that Janice's attitude was now different. She had called him at work and said she thought they maybe should talk. She didn't say what about, just that she had come to see it was necessary. He felt this was a shift, but maybe it was just wishful thinking on his account. He hadn't questioned her – he had just agreed and was hoping for the best.

After so much talk about France the week before, Andrew decided to call his sister, Karen. She had been surprised to hear from him after such a long time. They had chatted away for almost an hour. When she tried to remember the conversation later, she realized that they hadn`t really progressed further than what one could probably call "extended" small talk. Never mind, it was a start.

And Connor had paid Finn a visit. It had been quite a while since they had met and he noticed that he really missed their talks. He also felt he needed to share his pride in his new job with someone – and who better than Finn?

Potato Lasagne with Mince wrapped in Bacon

Tina had dropped her bag on the stairs, and as it had not been properly closed, she was busy picking up the contents when Andrew arrived on the scene. He noticed a glasses case, picked it up and handed it to her.

"This your case? I hadn`t noticed you wearing glasses."

"Back-up, only. I wear contact lenses, but you never know, do you?"

"Right – be prepared, as the boy scouts say."

"Were you a boy scout?"

"No, but that is their motto, isn`t it?"

"Your guess is as good as mine."

"These yours, too?"

"Oh my God, my nail scissors. I have been searching for those at home for ages."

"You`ll have to be careful with things like that when you fly to Greece. They search all bags, and they don`t allow potential weapons on board."

"I`ll remember that. Thanks."

"Oh, pepper spray! Is that legal?"

"It`s a non-toxic spray. Someone told me that was OK."

"Another back-up, then."

"You said it: be prepared."

"Do you go out much, then?"

"Not really. I meet up with a group from school every now and again, but I haven't done so often recently. We seem to be growing apart, somehow."

"I think I have seen you at the Dog & Collar, haven't I?"

"I don't recall. Sorry, that sounds terrible, doesn't it?"

"Not really. We didn't actually meet at any point. But I remember you were with a group of girls all kitted out for a night on the town."

"Oh yes. That was a few weeks ago. We had some drinks in the pub, and then they went off to some club."

They had arrived at the room where Connor and Heather were already sitting down together. At first, Andrew felt strange, he had thought she would want to stay in a team with him. They had got on so well last week. But then, talking to Tina was turning out easier than he had assumed. Why not play along?

"We have met before, you know," Heather had said as she walked over to Connor, who was, as always first to arrive.

"Really? I'm sorry, I don't remember. Do you have a relative at the hospice?"

"No. Fortunately, not. I work at the doctor's surgery in town. You have picked up some prescriptions for patients."

"Ah, I see. I don't do that often. I don't normally deal with anything on the medication side. I can't have been there often. You have a great memory for faces, it seems." (This was an attempt to quickly pull away from talking about medications)

"And names – you had your name tag on. But then, that is all part of my job. Remembering people, and their names."

"Part of my job, too. You're obviously better at it than I am."

"Probably just been at it longer. Had more practice. I have loads of kids` names to remember, as well. Plus, their parents. Plus, Jack`s colleagues, and their spouses and kids. No end of names to remember."

"You lead a busy life, it seems."

"Quite busy on the one hand, but on the other hand quite isolated." (she had no idea why she had suddenly felt the need to say that)

"You mean you live out of town?"

"In the suburbs, but not out in the wilds."

"The suburbs are normally quite lively, aren`t they?"

"We keep to ourselves, really."

"Through choice, you mean?"

"Yes, of course, through choice. What are you thinking of, Connor?"

"I just thought all families with kids hardly got a choice to keep themselves to themselves. Kids have a natural knack for hooking up with other kids."

"Emily is a bit of a loner."

"Not like her mum, then. She takes after her Dad, I suppose."

"Don`t suppose you remember, but we went to the same school, you know?" said Janice, approaching Lavinia on the stairs.

Lavinia wanted to say something about still having a good memory, but left it.

"Yes, I do remember actually. You were two years under me, weren`t you?"

"Good grief, you really do remember. Now, that`s a turn-up for the book. Who would have thought that."

"It`s not such a big deal, as you think. My brother was in your class."

"Ah, yes. Giles, wasn't it?"

"That's the one."

"Small world, isn't it?"

"Even smaller when you think that Tim was in my class."

"You know Tim?"

"Oh, everyone knew Tim."

"You obviously know we were together."

"Oh, everyone knew that."

"By the look on your face, you also know we are no longer together."

"Oh, everyone knows that."

Janice wished she could retreat and go home, but it was too late. They had arrived at the room, and disaster was in the making. The others had already teamed up for the evening. She was left with Lavinia. She realized that she had actually been dreading this set-up all along. And, this evening of all evenings, she had so wanted to remain with Connor. She had something important to tell him.

Rachel was eager to get started. The recipe today was rather more time-consuming than the others had been.

Three oven dishes were distributed. Onions and potatoes to peel - that was no longer a challenge. Layering of the ingredients was definitely manageable. The long cooking time – could be interesting as it would leave plenty of time for conversation. A full 45 minutes to clear up, set the table and await the feast.

"Well, if that doesn't impress them, I don't know what will," said Andrew

"Certainly looks impressive, I can tell you that. Looks very professional. By the way, I'm going to cook the stuffed peppers for my parents on Friday."

"So, it's your birthday on Friday, then?"

"You remembered! Goodness. Yes, it is. To be honest, I'm a bit nervous. If something can go wrong, it probably will."

"Rubbish. It'll be fine, I'm sure. What did your parents say when you said you were cooking for them instead of going out?"

"I haven't told them yet."

"You want to surprise them on the night?"

"No. I'm leaving the back door open in case I change my mind."

"You can't chicken out!"

"Wouldn't be the first time."

"But maybe the last time, was the last time."

"If only. I'm just not sure, and as long as I have an escape route…."

"Then tell them when you get home, and you're stuck."

"Andrew, may I ask you something?"

"Sure."

"I mean, would you? I just thought, could you? I mean, are you? Oh shit!"

"Out with it. What is it?"

"Are you doing anything on Friday? Could you maybe help me?"

"Erm…"

"No. OK, it is a bit too much to ask, isn't it?"

"It's OK. I have no fixed plans for Friday. I can come. I can help. Two free meals in one week – too good to miss, wouldn`t you say?"

Connor felt strangely affected by what Heather had said, so he decided to press her.

"So you feel isolated, even though you have a husband, and a daughter, and a busy work life? That`s some revelation, there, you know," he`d spurted it out before he`d really thought it through. He was sorry immediately.

Heather was actually quite a pleasant person – easy to talk to, amiable.

"You like to get to the bottom of things, don`t you?" she answered.

"I`m sorry if you think I`m interfering. I just find it unusual. I mean, I should be the one feeling isolated."

"Why should you feel isolated?"

Shit, this was going the wrong way. "I mean as opposed to you. You have everything all in one pile, don`t you?"

"Yes, all in one pile. That`s exactly it. Stuck in a pile, depending on where in the pile one is at a particular time, one can get to feel slightly smothered. Even if the pile is the right one. Do you get my meaning?"

"I think I do. You want a different order to your pile. More like piled up individually. Like next to each other? Like the pile waiting to be ironed, next to the pile waiting to be put back in the cupboard, unironed."

"No, that would be too apart. I don`t think I know what I mean, really. You`re right. I should be radiant with the luck I have, shouldn`t I?"

"Not if it doesn`t make you feel good."

"It does make me feel good. Just, well, smothered. Sometimes. A little. And then sometimes a little more. With no wriggle room for myself."

"Everyone needs to be able to have their own space. You don't have to be afraid to say that."

"It is one thing to articulate it. It is another to articulate it in such a way as for it not to be misunderstood."

"Where there's a will, there's a way."

"Mr Clever Clogs strikes again!"

"Yep. It is easy for me – I don't have to deal with it in real-time."

He went to check what the lasagne looked like, just to make sure Heather didn't ask any more questions.

Janice wasn't looking forward to a continuation of the conversation she had been having with Lavinia before they had started cooking. So, she tried to think of something else they could talk about.

"I read in the newspaper that our old Headmistress, Mrs Davenport, died last week."

"And I read in the newspaper that our old gym teacher, Miss Withering, got married last week. That's the difference between us. Always has been."

"I don't follow you."

"I look for the good news. You look for the bad news."

"I only said I had read it. There was no evaluation in my statement. I didn't say she has finally kicked the bucket, did I?"

"No. But then, I didn't say she's finally made it down the aisle, did I?"

"No. You didn't, and let's not forget not everyone makes it down the aisle."

"Oh shit. I'm sorry. I really don't know why I did that. I shouldn't have. I am sorry."

"I'm getting used to it by now."

"Don't be like that. I have said I'm sorry, and I really am."

"It still hurts. Tim leaving like that. It still hurts. I just don't get it."

"He hasn't got a new girlfriend. I can tell you that. I would know if he had."

"How the hell would you know that?"

"My husband, Ian, was in the same class as a work colleague of Tim's. They have a regular pub date every Thursday. They would have talked about it. That's how I knew you had separated."

"My God. The world gets smaller every time you look at it."

"Tim adores you. That's what they say. Always has done. From day one. Would do anything for you. They can't understand what he's done."

"I can't either."

The lasagne was ready.

It was excellent.

They all ate with a healthy appetite but couldn't manage all three dishes.

They offered Janice the lasagne which hadn't been started. She could warm it up for Dylan tomorrow. Janice refused, saying, "Dylan is staying with his grandparents for an extra night this week. Tim and I are going out for a meal together." There it was out. She had been longing to tell Connor all evening. She sent a coy look in Connor's direction, to which he gave her the thumbs up. Her smile broadened, which didn't get lost on the rest of the group.

It was decided that Lavinia, as the one with the most mouths to feed, should, in this case, take the lasagne home. She agreed – and she would put it under the grill.

Tina slipped a note into Andrew`s hand and he put it into his breast pocket. The *see you on Friday*, which he voiced in her direction as he left the room, also did not go unmissed by the rest of the group.

It wasn`t until after they had all left the room that Rachel realized that no-one had asked what was to be cooked next week.

Rachel`s Realm

I knew it all along! thought Rachel as she turned the key in the lock. *I knew that they knew each other. I could sense it from the start. Now, isn`t that strange; that it should take five weeks for them to openly voice it? Definitely a whiskey ginger evening tonight.*

Lavinia and Janice were apparently at the same school, and the other coincidences in their lives were really quite remarkable. Lavinia knew all along why Janice was so down; how come she hadn`t spoken to her before? They had almost avoided each other for the previous four evenings. Mind you, if the truth were to out, she, Rachel, would also try and avoid someone like Janice. Her negative slant to everything was rather difficult to accept. But then, as far as she could catch the conversation, it would seem that her boyfriend had not been gone for long. She was still suffering from the blow. It did seem that Lavinia`s message about him not having a new girlfriend did bring a little twinkle to the rather sad eyes to which they had all become accustomed. We`ll know more next week, though. She said she was meeting, no, actually going out for a meal with Tim tomorrow. That look she sent Connor was a real give-away. What has he been up to? That lad is an absolute mystery. How can he possibly have fixed up such a meeting?

And even he had known Heather before they started the course. Imagine that! And neither had said anything until tonight. But then, I thought I recognized her from somewhere, hadn`t thought about the doctor`s surgery. That would explain how she manages to speak so calmingly to people, though, wouldn`t it? Who would have guessed what she had bottled up inside her? Who would have thought that she felt so uneasy with her life? Who could possibly imagine that someone in such stable and indeed loving surroundings could perceive those as smothering? It was so funny to hear her talking about laundry to Connor – what a comparison! Her life with a pile of laundry! You don`t say things like that to just anyone, do you? Or do you? Was it the non-intimacy that made it easier? After all, Connor knows neither Heather`s husband, nor her daughter. He certainly is able to extract information from others with such ease that people don`t realize how much they are revealing about themselves. Here, I am saying, with such ease, that actually he can be quite blunt when he feels it is necessary.

Sitting in the comfort of her home, sipping her whiskey ginger, Rachel felt a pang of pity when she thought of Connor. He had said that he didn't have any contact with his parents for almost five years. How often had she now asked herself just how on earth something like that could happen to such an appealing lad?

Her Mince Stew recipe for next week was for him. For him and his parents. She sincerely hoped he would manage to fix whatever was amiss.She suddenly felt a little lonely as she thought about her own two children. This feeling didn`t last long – they were coming home at the weekend, and she would be cooking for them. She would be cooking for Katrina`s birthday.

Apropos birthday: what was going on in Tina`s life? It was her birthday this week, as well. She had said she was cooking on Friday for her parents. Hadn`t told them yet, of course. Then, she even invited Andrew along. My goodness me, that was a turn-up for the books (she should go red in embarrassment at the thought of how many such conversations she had actually overheard). Well, Tina had actually made a decision and seen it through.

So good of Andrew to play along, although he did play it down quite. Never mind, if something comes of it, all's well and good. It is such a pity that the girls he invites home don`t seem to be as impressed with his cooking as he wishes. Poor chap, maybe he`s inviting the wrong type of girl – looking for the wrong characteristics, picking up the wrong signals. Had he seen Tina before? Was he much more sly than one imagined at first glance?

Would it be meddling where she shouldn`t if she interfered with this development? Surely, Connor would be a better match for Tina. How come she hadn`t asked Connor to help her?

He wasn't that much younger than her, and age differences weren't such a big deal these days anyway.

As she finished off her whiskey ginger, she weighed up her options. It didn't take her long to realize that she really didn't have any real options – the ball was definitely on the other side of the court and not on hers.

Mince Stew

Connor had called his parents and spoken to them on the phone. It had been five years since they had had any contact whatsoever. That considered, the call had gone well. Rather staccato at first, but gradually getting better. He had invited them to his new flat. They should come on Saturday, and he would cook a meal for them. They had accepted. He only hoped the meal would be to their liking, he had completely forgotten to ask last week what it was Rachel had thought up for him. But here he was, on their last evening, ready to go. First there, as usual, he greeted Rachel, sat down, and waited for Heather.

Andrew had been to Tina's on the Friday before the last evening of their course.

He had gone into town in the afternoon and bought her a book as a birthday present. It was a travel book on Greece with loads of photos, plenty of information about Greece and the Greeks, and even some tourist phrases for her to learn. He hoped she had already told her parents about her holiday. But then, he decided, if she hadn't, she would have her hand forced – she hadn't minded Connor doing that, so he hoped it was okay for him to do it, as well.

They had cooked together and they had eaten with her parents. Who, it seemed, had been surprised to be invited to a meal in their own home, and were more than pleasantly surprised to have her bring a man-friend home. It had been a most enjoyable evening. Not even disturbed by the fact that she hadn't told her parents about her holiday plans. She had booked, but wanted to tell them during their meal. They were, of course, surprised that Andrew already knew but were quite obviously resigned to the fact that this was the future

He greeted Rachel and Connor as he entered the room and then he looked around for Tina.

Lavinia had decided YOLO was for her.

After declining the Team Leader job, and then asking to go part-time she had been summoned to the boss's office. With an uneasy feeling, she had gone there only to find out that he was at a loss to understand why she had reacted the way she had. He questioned her at length. He was disappointed in her reaction to the promotion. He had waited for the position to come up, knowing it was perfect for her, that she was the most suitable candidate. Why hadn't she gone for it? He had thought she'd been waiting for it, as well. Then she asked to go part-time. Well, he wanted her to know they were sad she had made this decision. They would prefer to keep her (OMG, she thought, they're going to sack me!) so could she explain her decisions and include the expectations of her work life to such an extent that he could assess the situation correctly and make her an appropriate offer? They didn't want to lose such a valued employee.

Then today, she had been summoned into his office again. He had an offer to make. She could be promoted to the next tier. She would have to change departments, but

the new job would bring more responsibility and more money. The bonus here being, with fixed hours. She should think about it and let him know within 24 hours if this was what she wanted. He hoped so, he couldn't hold the offer open for long.

YOLO – She didn't need 24 hours, she had to go for this.

She looked radiant as she arrived in the room. Looked around, greeted the two men, greeted Rachel, and sat down to wait for Janice.

Heather was at peace with herself. Not yet at peace with Eamon, but she knew how she would handle it. It had to be done carefully, after all, he was her boss, and she didn't want to lose her job. She was glad to have this evening away from everyone at home and at work and had looked forward to it all day. She realized now that love could be smothering and space was needed. She had created some in being here every Wednesday, Jack had found some with his creative writing and they were all better for it. They had opened up, and come closer. Connor made a sign as she arrived. She greeted everyone and walked over towards him.

Janice was the one with the biggest piece of news. She couldn't wait to tell everyone. There was a skip in her pace that was immediately noticeable. She as good as ignored everyone in the room as she approached Lavinia, then she realized what she was doing, stopped in her tracks, made an extravagant hand gesture, and with a "Hi everyone," sat down.

Tina was just a little late. She had just come from a viewing. It was the second one this week. On a high after the success of Friday evening, she had actually entered the estate agent's on Saturday and registered herself as "searching" for property. There were some really interesting ones on offer.

It would seem all were ready to get started.

"What are we cooking today?" they all asked simultaneously.

"Mince Stew – this can be prepared in advance and placed on the table for eating whenever the guests are ready. Absolutely no time restrictions for pre-dinner conversations and no stress for the host as everything can be finished in advance."

Rachel placed the vegetables on the tables.

Potatoes, carrots, red peppers, and green peppers. All to be prepared, as learnt, and cut into small pieces.

40 minutes would be needed for the stew to be cooked.

Only after the 40 minutes should the sour cream be added.

Delicious on an autumn evening, or a winter evening, or a Saturday afternoon after football, or whenever.

Also good to prove to your parents you can cook without going over the top.

Rachel wished Connor luck from the bottom of her heart.

Andrew and Tina were lost in conversation.

"I wish to thank you so much for coming over on Friday."

"I enjoyed it. Your parents are really cool. So interested in everything."

"They were certainly interested in you. I think they may have the wrong impression about our relationship, though."

"Isn`t that what you wanted?"

"Touchè. It was, I suppose."

"I tagged along with it. It is okay with me." (*Tag-along, why had he used that word? Should he tell her?*)

"Well, double thanks then. It has made things so much easier for me. They are suddenly so open to me turning my life around – upside down, even."

"While you`re about it, you should consider changing your girly group. They don`t know how to appreciate your company."

"I don`t follow. Do you know them?"

"That time when I saw you at the pub, you were in a group with four other girls. Then you all went off to a club. I was in a group of five guys, we thought it would be a good idea to follow you."

"Really!"

"Yep. Then, at the club, you were no longer there. Only four girls – and us five guys. It was like playing musical chairs, and I was left without a chair. We almost met then. When we asked where the fifth girl was, they just said, Oh, tag-along Tina? She never joins in. She just tags-along for a while. We humour her."

"What!"

"You don't need them, Tina. You are about to start your own life. Leave them be."

"Where would I be without you?"

Connor and Heather were equally intense in their discourse:

"I hope this works out. I've invited my parents over for a Saturday evening meal."

"It'll be fine, you'll see."

"Can't help feeling a little uneasy."

"That's normal in your situation."

"My situation is very far from normal. You forget I'm the isolated one."

"Things can change, if you let them."

"You fixed your pile of washing then, have you?"

"I'm well on the way. The laundry is in the machine, and when it comes out, I'll sort everything differently; some things will be hung up to dry, some will go in the tumble-dryer, and some will just be folded up. But in the end, all will meet up in the cupboard where they belong."

"We're quite philosophical today, aren't we?"

"Thoughtful, I'd call it. Has a better ring to it."

"Well, my washing is still in the washing machine. It's still spinning."

"Hang it out to dry on the line. It smells fresher that way."

"You're fooling with me now, aren't you? But OK, I can go along with that." (In fact, he preferred it that way. Then things didn't get too close to him having to explain anything)

"You're okay, Connor. Don't let anyone tell you any different."

Even Lavinia and Janice were chatting away – albeit not quite so amicably.

"How did the evening out go?"

"Better than expected."

"Oh, my God, Janice. Don't start like that."

"What's wrong, now?"

"Did it go well or not?"

"Well. Very well."

"Then say so, for goodness sake. You're enough to test the Holy Father."

"We're getting back together."

"What?!"

"Tim is moving back in at the weekend."

"You mean, he's coming home?"

"Yes, you could say that."

"I would say that."

"Dylan is over the moon."

"And you?"

"Me, too."

"Then say so, for crying out loud."

"I am really excited."

"Me, too."

"Why would you be excited that Tim is moving, er, coming home?"

"I'm excited because I have been promoted. Promoted to a job I can handle alongside my family."

"Congratulations. I am sure you deserve it!"

"Of course I do ……. Christ, Janice, you can be annoying, you know."

The stew was ready.

Just as they sat down to eat the stew, the door opened, and a reporter and a photographer from the *Town Chronicle* walked in. They were going to do a report on some of the new developments at the Community Centre, and this was going to be one of the main features.

James, the roving reporter, asked questions such as:

"What made you decide on this course?"

"What have you learnt over the last six evenings?" and *"Would you recommend this type of course to others?"*

They were all very coy in their answers. It was one thing to open up to this group. It was completely another, to be honest with the rest of the world – or, in this case, the locals.

One thing they all agreed on was that they would definitely sign-up for the next course if Rachel was willing to offer one.

Hair was adjusted, clothes were pulled into place, smiles were pinned on.

Cheese! A great number of photos were taken.

The reporter and his photographer then left the group to enjoy their meal.

"I didn't bring any bubbly with me as I assumed it wasn't allowed here," said Lavinia

There she goes again, assumptions, assumptions, thought Andrew

"So, I'd like to invite you all for a drink at The Woolpack after we finish here this evening. I have something to celebrate."

"Brilliant idea. I do, too," said Heather

"Couldn't have put it better myself!" said Janice

"We should make it a regular date," said Tina

"The Six Pack at the Woolpack it is," said Connor.

Suddenly, it seemed almost at the same time, they all remembered that actually there were seven of them. Would Rachel come along, as well? Where would they all be today if it hadn't been for her offering this course?

Rachel's Realm

Rachel had felt slightly put out that they hadn't thought of including her right away, but then she had, after all, been the instructor, or maybe more a facilitator. At least, they had remembered in time. Although her first reaction was to accept and go along, she had decided not to.

Isn't it supposed to be best to stop when you're on a high? That was how she felt at that moment – on a high. She had reached a target, one which she didn't even have when she had entered that kitchen on the first evening of the course.

She had experienced scenes unfolding in front of her and was proud of her part in it. She had to admit to herself that parts of her experiences were possibly not so kosher; after all, she had eavesdropped on personal conversations. But then again, how could she not have overheard? And, most important, she had not intervened. She had let things roll and had let fate do its job.

She had seen them develop from six adults flung together to do some casual cooking to being a group of adults relaxed and open in their interaction. Indeed, friendships had been started and were being strengthened.

She had seen them hiding from themselves, shielding feelings, running away from responsibility, and literally kidding themselves. And now she saw them at ease with themselves, individually and within the group.

Even Connor had seemed to be more relaxed. Isn't there a special one in every group? Connor, the youngest, the most inquisitive, the most sensitive, the most mysterious.

Rachel arrived home feeling well-pleased with herself. She felt she had really achieved something. Maybe it wasn't explicitly her doing, but without her it couldn't have happened. Each participant had played a role, one that mostly they didn't know they were playing, but it had worked. Each participant had undergone a change during the six weeks.

Not only their cooking skills had been upended, but parts of their lives had been as well.

Even for Rachel – yes, she also had every reason to feel elated, for she too had something to look forward to. Edmond was so grateful to her for stepping in and running the course for them that he had invited her for a meal. They were going to one of the most exquisite restaurants in town. On Friday evening at 7.00 pm, he would pick her up.

Just goes to show, with an open mind, an interest in others, and a dose of empathy, the world offers you a new edition of your personal cookery book.

PART 2:

The Six Pack at the Woolpack

2/ONE

The Woolpack

At first glance, the Woolpack was an unpretentious pub, and only on closer examination did one find it something to write home about. It stood, as it had in some form or another for over 300 years, on an island as the main road through the town forked around it. As this alone made car parking extremely difficult, if it weren't for the municipal car park 300m down the road and the supermarket car park around the corner, one could class it as impossible. This made what is known as casual trade a constant battle. Hardly a visitor would simply drop by perchance. Fortunately for the new landlord, the pub was of excellent repute and was a favourite drinking hole for many local residents. It was readily frequented at lunchtime by the bankers and entrepreneurs of the thriving mid-England town in which it stood.

It was easily identifiable as a pub with its mural of a flock of six sheep on the wall between the two upstairs windows. This eye-catching element was particularly important as the entrance was on the left side of the building, somewhat out of sight. Anyone foreign to the area would have to go in search of the door. The search was well worth it, though.

Once inside, one was met with an atmospheric warmth that only a traditional English pub can offer. It comprised two rooms: a middle-sized one to the left and a larger one to the right of the entrance area. The smaller of the two had been transformed into a pub-type restaurant; pub-type being no tablecloths, wooden chairs with no padding, salt, pepper, and vinegar placed mid-table, and a blackboard stating the Menu of the Day. The menu was changed every day, but an observant eye (or a regular visitor) could quickly recognise that it was merely rotated—there were eight dishes which the chef, Danny, could conjure up; however, praise be where praise is due—he did his job well and was appreciated accordingly.

The room on the right-hand side was obviously more the area for drinking. A sandwich could be had here if the restaurant was full or if time was short, but in general, here the locals met for a pint. Renovations here had been costly but necessary. They had also been carefully done with a passion for pub-goers. The open fireplace remained a centrepiece; it had been modernised and was now a more efficient wood-burner, but it had kept its old inglenook look. The small round tables, which were dotted nearby, all had four chairs each and were of mock mahogany; this did not make the effect dark, rather it contrasted with the light-filled room which was intensified by the two strategically placed partitions with stained glass elements. Further away from the fireplace, the tables were lower and chairs more comfortable, more lounge-like. Any drinker had a definite choice of venue within the venue.

The original bar counter had been kept and sanded down to a pale brown. The back bar fitting accommodated a mass of spirits and wines and was well-illuminated to ensure everyone knew what was available. The bar walk was tiled in a dark brown and gave way to a patterned carpet, ready to soak up any stains. All in all, quite homely.

It was in this pub that the so-called "Six Pack" met every Wednesday at 6.00 pm. It was always interesting to see how punctual they all were— all six of them. It sometimes seemed as if they treated it as a timetabled session. They were an unusual group of four women and two men and always sat at the same table, which had a "reserved" card on it, placed there by Toby without fail by 5.30pm at the latest. They sat at the large, round Britannia table in the bay window in the far corner of the lounge bar, which was still coined the "Smoke Room".

Toby was the new landlord. It had always been his aim to run a pub when he retired from the army. He had been over the moon when he heard that the landlord of the Woolpack was planning to sell up and had been quick off the mark to ensure he threw his towel in the ring early. He had been successful and now poured all his energy into making this enterprise something to be proud of. So much so that his wife had left him and was now sunning herself in Spain with her latest conquest. He wouldn't want her back now anyway, he told himself over and over. She was collateral damage as far as he was concerned. He now had Jack to help out. He had advertised for a "Man Friday" and had found a superb example of one. Jack was strong, a dab hand at DIY, reliable, honest, jolly, empathic—just the kind of gregarious person every pub needs. He had even agreed to move into the flat above the outbuilding at the back of the pub. With Danny as chef and the two barmaids, Sadie and Cath, he had a pub crew par excellence. Toby could hardly believe his good fortune. Lady Luck had certainly served him a good hand. With a rather smug look on his face, he greeted Connor.

Connor was always the first of the Six Pack group to arrive. He was a resident carer at the local hospice and was a secretive kind of chap in many ways. Always ready to chat but never giving too much away. Toby only knew where he worked because one of the other locals had told him that he had been a most wonderful carer for his mother before she passed away.

As Connor placed his coat over the back of the chair, Tina arrived. Toby knew her from the bank. She was a strange girl—no, woman, one should say. She looked much younger than she was and always seemed just slightly undecided as to what to do. She always hesitated before doing anything; just like now, she was about to sit opposite Connor and then stopped, just for a second, only to decide to stay with her first choice of chair after all.

Next in was Andrew—grumpy again. Toby couldn`t get his head around this lad; he always seemed to be angry with something or someone. Somehow, though, he did brighten up every week and always left the pub in a much better mood than he had arrived in. He sat down next to Tina, flashed a half smile at Connor, and grinned at Tina.

"Hi, everyone," came from the door—it was Heather, the receptionist from the doctor`s surgery. Toby liked her; she was always so friendly and somehow so happy. She seemed to have a never-ending supply of smiles. Toby often wondered how on earth she fitted into this group of six.

The missing two, Janice and Lavinia, arrived together—they mostly did. Toby knew them both as partners of other regulars. Lavinia's husband, Ian, was a staunch regular. He came every week with his pals, though never with his wife. Janice's boyfriend, Tim, often came with a group from work, though not every week—maybe once a month.

As they sat down with the others at the table, Toby stood behind the counter and waited for their order. It would be two pints of bitter, one white wine, one gin and tonic, one lager and lime, and one lemonade and lime. Always was. He waited all the same. He waited to see whose turn it was to pay, who would step up to the counter and place the first order of the evening. He was putting his money on Andrew—must be his turn again by now.

Yes, he was right—Andrew it was, and the order was as always. A landlord always knows his regulars, doesn't he?

Toby actually enjoyed them coming to the pub. It was fascinating to see—and hear—how they interacted. As long as there were groups like this around, he felt the world would manage to survive what fate had to throw at it. He knew about fate, and he knew what it could do to you and with you. His life hadn't always been easy, not least due to his choice of wife. He joined the army straight from school, had spent time abroad, spent time in conflicts, and had learnt more than enough about the depths of human nature. He'd left the army feeling he had done his duty, done his bit. He was ready to enjoy life—he wanted to run a pub. Couldn't be too hard, wasn't rocket science, was it? It had been harder than he thought, but failure was not an option. He wanted to see a different side of human nature. Oh, yes, there were times when he thought, my God, don't they know when enough is enough. And there had been times when he had had to refuse someone another drink. There had been times when he had had to intervene in fights, but this was all nothing compared to some of the things he had experienced in the army. He had drawn a line under his army past, now revelling in his new life as the landlord of an urban pub, a popular urban pub, a pub where the locals came and went, and came again, where they felt at home and well looked after. That's how he saw it. He wasn't past his sell-by date yet, he had plenty more to offer and he was glad they were part of his life. He relished evenings like Wednesdays, when groups like this Six Pack, as they called themselves, came and simply enjoyed each other's company and the atmosphere of his pub.

2/TWO

Tina's Troubles

Tina had picked her seat opposite Connor for a reason. She wanted to be able to look him in the eye. She needed to be able to see him when he reacted to what she had to say. It was always easier to discuss things with someone sitting opposite you; she knew this from one of her training courses at the bank. Today, she needed to interact with him. She felt he would be the one to be most understanding, and most helpful. For help was what she was after; how else could she cope?

Andrew arrived and, of course, sat next to her. He always did. Not that she was complaining—she actually liked him a lot. He had been the first man she had taken home to meet her parents. They had misinterpreted the situation, but that was what she had wanted. She had wanted to make a statement; he had played along. Hard to accept it was a mere two months ago. He was indeed a good friend. Maybe she should offer to pay his round today; after all, he didn't earn much and was probably the one with the least amount at his disposal. No, better not, don't want to hurt his feelings.

The other three members of the group trickled in and took their seats. It never ceased to astound Tina how much she looked forward to these meetings, and she was sure the feeling was mutual. It simply felt right. So much of a routine had already developed that Andrew (who knew it was his turn) didn't even have to ask what everyone wanted to drink—he knew. They all just confirmed they were in for the usual, and off he went to the bar.

When he returned to the table with the drinks, Tina lost no time. "Cheers" all round. Now, she had to get this off her chest as quickly as possible:

"There's something I just have to ask you all. I don't understand what is happening at work, and it is driving me crazy. All of a sudden, things seem to have gone completely out of control. My boss, Simon, has turned on me. I can`t do anything right in his eyes. This is so out of character; he was always so reasonable with me. He just jumps at me for no reason whatsoever. Last week, he even left me out of the team meeting. He said he had sent me an invitation, but he hadn`t. I really didn`t get one. I asked for the morning off yesterday to go and see a house in town which has just come on the market. He refused to let me go! I only wanted two hours, but he said there was too much work and I hadn`t even completely finished my tasks from last week. This is so not true."

Tears began to appear in Tina's eyes—Andrew, to her right, put his hand on her arm, and Heather, to her left, stroked her shoulder.

"Why is he doing this to me? This morning, I saw him in the rec room with a couple of colleagues down from Head Office, and when they saw me, they looked away. I`m sure they were talking about me. This is all so horrible. I haven`t been any different, done anything different. In fact, if anything, I have tried harder to be collegial. I've tried to help the new clerk find her feet and even undertook to do some of her tasks as she couldn`t manage to finish them on time. What have I done wrong?"

A silence fell over the group. No one really wanted to be the one to break it. Heather then said, "Is he new in the job?"

"No, he`s been my boss for the last three years. He came from some building society, fresh into branch banking. But we never had a problem, never a harsh word, never a complaint about my work, nothing of the sort. I do have slightly different responsibilities now that Stella has gone, but nothing that really interferes with our working together. You know, I think it was even him that recommended me for the extra duties. It really just does not add up. He seems to be moving the goalposts all the time. Stella didn`t get on with him; I think he didn`t like her. He seemed to be watching out for her to make mistakes, and he was really nasty about her behind her back. She never knew, though. To her face, he was always so pleasant. I gave him a nasty look once when he was being so overly nice to her about something, and he just smirked back at me."

Lavinia's face changed; she suddenly remembered a course she had been on. She asked, "Do you have an anti-bullying policy at the bank?"

"I don`t know. I`ve never thought about it. Don`t think anyone has ever mentioned it, though. What exactly would that be? What exactly is bullying? Do you think my boss is a bully?"

"I went to a training session about 'Bullying in the Workplace' once, actually about anti-bullying, of course, and when you were listing all the things that are happening to you, it began to sound familiar. It is almost a classic case! I just can`t figure out yet why he has suddenly picked you. After all that time, did you not notice anything before?"

Janice had been particularly pensive and now asked, "We have such a policy at the Town Hall, and the first paragraph is a definition of bullying. Certainly sounds like your boss fits the bill to me. He seems to tick all the boxes."

Tina looked at Connor, willing him to speak.

He did, "I think we may be taking this a bit too far. I can remember when I started at the Hospice, I had a really hard time. The Matron was always questioning what I was doing; nothing was ever good enough. She watched me like a hawk, waiting for me to make a mistake. She gave me all the difficult patients and all the worst shifts. I was definitely never her flavour of the month. But, do you know what? She wasn't bullying me. She was just ensuring I was right for the job. That I was up to it. She had looked at me and thought I was one of those who gave up when things got tough. She wanted things to get tough, just to see if I would give up. She was actually helping me."

Janice showed a little impatience. "Oh, come on, Connor. Listen to what Tina is saying. He isn`t trying to help her. He has been her Manager for three years, he`s not testing her, is he? Whatever he is doing, he`s taking it to the next level, isn`t he?"

"Tell us, why did your colleague, did you say Stella, leave?"

"She came back from a holiday in Cornwall and asked for a transfer to a branch down there. My guess is, she met someone from there while she was on holiday and wanted to move there."

"Or, she had decided not to stay in the old environment any longer for some other reason. When did she leave?"

"She left about four weeks ago."

Lavinia beamed. "That's it. He didn't lose any time, did he? Don't you all see the picture here? The bully lost his victim, so he went looking for a new one and found one."

"Are you saying I should ask for a transfer?"

Andrew had absolutely no experience whatsoever in this field, but he felt it was time he joined in. "Tina, no. You can't give in to someone like that. You have to confront him. Tell him how you feel, tell him you won't take it. Be proactive."

Heather didn't agree. "No, that won't work. If he really is a bully, he will only be happy that you feel bad. It won't help at all. Have you spoken to anyone else about this? To your parents? Or to one of your colleagues?"

"No, I haven't. My parents wouldn't understand, and to be honest, I feel a little ashamed. Too ashamed to talk to my colleagues about it." She downed the rest of her drink.

Lavinia announced it was her round and got up to get the drinks. "Same as always, everyone?"

Tina was on a low. "No, I think I need something stronger. A gin and tonic, please."

Toby was surprised as Lavinia gave him the order. "Two pints of bitter, two gin and tonics, a white wine, and a lemonade and lime, please." Something was amiss at the table, he thought. But he said nothing, of course. Always the good innkeeper, observant, but mum.

Back at the table with the drinks, Lavinia heard Janice claim, "from the top."

She said, "Before you all go any further, I have to tell you one thing we were told at the course. Bullying is not against the law. Harassment is, but not bullying. Tina, first you should check the grievance policy that your employer has. Once you know that, you can approach the HR department and talk to them."

Andrew was feeling protective. "Will they do anything, though? They'll probably just talk to the bloke and he`ll deny everything and things will just get worse for Tina. We can`t be responsible for letting that happen."

Tina took a rather large gulp of her drink. "It does feel good to talk to you all. It makes me feel better now, but, I`m not looking forward to going into work tomorrow now. How can I face him after what you have all said? Maybe it would just be easier to apply for a transfer. Oh my God."

Connor was ready with his response. "Stop! Stop right there. If he is a bully—and maybe I was wrong not to see it earlier, you can`t just leave. If you leave, he will just move on to his next victim. Actually you do have to give someone the heads up on this – but, but until you have enough facts, you have to stay under the radar. He mustn`t suspect you`re planning anything."

"Connor, we have to consider Tina`s feelings here. Be a little more sympathetic."

"Andrew, I am sympathetic to Tina`s situation. You know that Tina, don`t you? (Tina nodded, not particularly enthusiastically, but a nod all the same). You have to ask yourself, can I face up to him? If push comes to shove, have I got the strength to stand up to him? If you haven`t, you have to apply for the transfer and leave everyone else to fight their own battles. However, if you do have that strength – he paused, very dramatically – you have to prepare your case well, talk to HR, defend yourself (and others), and ensure he is the one to get the transfer. It ain`t over till it`s over. That`s how I see it."

Tina placed her glass on the table and stared at Connor. She knew it was right to sit opposite him, she had watched him while he spoke. He meant it, he really did. He thought she was strong. He really did.

Did she think she was?

"Thank you. To all of you," she said. "This has helped me a lot. One thing I do know is I am not going to work tomorrow. I will use the time to think about what I should do."

Lavinia knew this was the right thing to do, although it also fitted into what she had heard during the course. Bullying leads to increased sick leave, and bullying makes the victim ill over time.

Janice promised to check the anti-bullying charter at work the following day and to let Tina know what they recommended should be done.

Heather was heartbroken that Tina should be going through this and felt totally out of her depth. How on earth could she help?

Connor kissed Tina on the cheek as they said their good-byes. He'd never done that before but he felt the need to give an extra portion of understanding today.

And Andrew had a free day tomorrow so he offered to come round and sit with Tina while she did her thinking. He would gather as much info as possible in the meantime.

Toby watched them leave the pub together. Tina, so obviously upset, and everyone so determined to help and give her support. He'd overheard a lot of the conversation. They really didn't realise how the acoustics of the bay window worked. He had heard the word "bully" and "bullying" a number of times. He didn't know anything about bullying in civilian life, but in the army, it was rife. He thought,

We just called it something different and had a different way of dealing with it. Army life was very different to civilian life.

Thank Goodness he was where he was, as he contemplated how one should actually deal with bullies.

Were they actually the strong ones? In a school playground situation, maybe, just maybe. But in later life? From his point of view, it must surely be a sign of weakness. Playing over, hiding something so that other`s wouldn`t see it. In the school playground the bully found himself (or herself) playmates to support him/her. That made them a group and thus more visible. Then he remembered the group that came in Saturdays, they were always on about how they had fooled "Old Barry," as they called him. They were definitely outgrown schoolkids, hadn`t quite got beyond the playground bully act. He had no idea who this Old Barry was, so he couldn`t have helped even if he had thought he should. Wasn`t that a blessing in disguise?

"Two brown ales, please Toby," he heard from the other side of the counter. Whoops, he was losing his knack. Normally he could contemplate matters and take in the surroundings at the same time. Many a time he had been preoccupied with something, or other, but still managed to note when more drinks could be sold. Seems this bullying – of Tina – was getting to him more than he thought.

What the hell can one do? What should one do? There must be some help on the internet. Some help line, or other. Hope they find it. Nothing he could do to help, was there? Did that make him part of the problem? Not doing anything to help, could be seen as aiding the culprit, couldn`t it? He had to stop this train of thought. Not because he wanted to, simply because a group of ten arrived. They had obviously come from somewhere, possibly the fitness centre, and were quite loud. They wouldn`t want to hang about waiting for their drinks. He was back in his element. This was something he could handle. Bullying was not. He could close his eyes to it, as so many people do. In fact, that was the only plausible thing to do, wasn`t it?

2/THREE

Meanwhile, at the "B" s

The doorbell rang, and Tina`s mum answered it. It was Andrew. She was surprised to see him but didn`t let on, just invited him in. She liked Andrew; he was such a polite young man. He called her Mrs B, which always made her smile. There was no smile on his face this morning, though. He was obviously troubled in some way. She did hope that they hadn`t had a fall-out. That really would be such a pity, she thought as she watched him walk up the stairs to Tina`s room.

"I`ll bring you both some tea."

Tina was lying on the bed, curled up like a foetus. Normally she would have made an effort to be dressed smartly and put on a touch of make-up, but today was different. She couldn`t be bothered. She was clothed in what her parents called her home-dress: baggy tracksuit trousers and an even baggier T-shirt. She had been crying and made no attempt to hide the fact as Andrew knocked and walked into her room. Her mobile phone lay on the desk to the right of the laptop. The last call made had been to the bank to tell them she was sick and wouldn`t be in today, and probably not tomorrow either. Fortunately, it had been Anita who answered the phone and not her boss, Simon. Tina had no idea how she would have reacted if he had answered. Anita had been understanding and wished her a speedy recovery. There, her luck had run out. When she turned on her laptop and checked her emails, there was one from Simon. He wanted to remind her that—although she was officially on sick leave—she shouldn`t forget that the quarterly report was due in on Monday. Hence the tears.

Andrew sat down on the bed and held Tina in his arms. There was so much warmth in this scene that it seemed almost impossible that these two were not lovers. They weren`t. That threshold had not been crossed; in fact, it didn`t even seem to exist. They were just glad to have each other as friends—very close friends. Tina showed Andrew the email, and he stood up, fighting back his anger at this Simon chap. He took a deep breath and sat down at the desk. He was sitting there as Mrs B walked in with the tea. The tears in Tina's eyes didn't go unmissed, but Mrs B said nothing, just put the tea down on the desk, smiled caringly at her daughter, and walked back out through the door.

"Come on, this won't do," said Andrew. "We have work to do. Get yourself over here."

Tina obeyed. They spent the next five hours milling over websites and internet forums, gathering info on bullying. The more they read, the more they realised that this was what was happening at the bank. This was what Tina was having to suffer. At the end of their session, they had decided that Tina would need more time off than the two days which were planned so far. Tina called Dr Brewer's surgery and made an appointment for Friday afternoon. She hoped he could think of some reason to sign her off sick for a while longer.

Andrew came over on Friday morning as well. This visit he used to re-build Tina's self-confidence. She had never been the most confident of people, always hesitant to decide anything, never really feeling she had the right answers. Now this whole business was dragging her even further down. It was painful to watch. Andrew talked incessantly, pleading with her and speaking of all the things she could be proud of in her life. He made some progress, although not half as much as he had wanted, and probably only a third of what was going to be needed to counter this attack.

Mr and Mrs B still couldn't fathom out what was going on but were pleased to note that whatever they talked about, Tina was better in herself. She had made an appointment at the doctor's for the afternoon— for a short second, they had even considered that maybe they were to be grandparents soon. They had brushed that aside, albeit hesitantly. Andrew was to return in the evening, and the two of them were going to cook dinner for them all. This was just how they had foreseen life—so cosy. So pleased were they that they had called Ted and Jean, their friends across the road, and arranged to go over to play cards after dinner to leave the two "youngsters" alone. They had known Ted and Jean all their married life. Tina had never got on well with their son, Bill. Bill would have made a fine match as the families were so close. He was married now and lived on the other side of town with his wife and baby boy and worked as a manager at the DIY store on Westcote Avenue. Now, there was a coincidence which Mrs B saw as a sign—that was exactly the DIY store where Andrew worked. Of course, she hadn`t mentioned it to Andrew or to Tina, but both she and Mr B had made a mental note—sometimes fate needs a little push in the right direction, doesn`t it?

2/FOUR
Janice's Jubilation?

It was Wednesday, so Toby placed the "reserved" card on the table in the bay window at 5.30 pm, as usual. He recalled to memory the scenario that had played out before his eyes the week before and wondered how the mood would be today. Maybe all was well again. One can hope.

Such a strange group of people, he wondered what it was that bound them together. There was such an intimacy around the group, although it was plainly obvious that there was not a love affair in sight. Except maybe a flickering of a slightly deeper kind when it came to Tina and Andrew. Poor Tina, he sure hoped she was okay again. Toby had no time to dwell on the matter, though. He had office business to deal with before the evening crowd arrived. He hardly noticed how the time sped past and was genuinely surprised when Connor appeared at the door of the pub.

Connor sat down and placed his coat on the back of the chair; his bottom had not hit the chair seat before Heather arrived and sat down next to him. Andrew and Tina arrived not only at the same time but obviously together. There was a new quality to their relationship which was apparent not only to Toby but to the other two as well. As they saw Lavinia and Janice coming through the doorway, Tina gave Andrew her purse. He checked with Connor and Heather that they were on track for the usual order and walked towards the two newcomers, who also confirmed they wanted the same as always. They were, however, slightly surprised it was Andrew asking. Had he come into some money? It wasn't his turn again already, of that they were sure. Naturally, Toby said nothing as Andrew ordered the drinks; he said nothing about it being him ordering and he would be damned if he would mention that he had seen Tina give him her purse.

Back at the table, Tina had begun to give a summary of her week:

"I haven't been at work at all this week. I took last Thursday and Friday off and went to see the doctor on Friday afternoon. He was very understanding and has written me off sick for two weeks to clear my thoughts. I have until next Wednesday to sort myself out. Andrew has been such a help, I don't know what I would have done without him. We found all sorts of information from websites on the internet. We have now definitely come to the conclusion that what I experienced was first-rate bullying. You were right, Janice, he really does tick all the boxes. You just wouldn't believe how widespread bullying is. I thought it was only me that was suffering such behaviour. That alone made me feel a lot better. Not that I am any stronger in myself — I still can't face up to him. I just can't."

She had to struggle a little with some tears which, in spite of all her effort, were hovering on the surface, ready to flow at any point. Relief came in the form of Andrew with the drinks.

"Cheers!"

"Was the doctor able to help in any other way, other than giving you some time off work?" asked Heather, who sincerely hoped that Dr Brewer, her once-time lover, had been able to rise to the occasion and give her some useful advice.

"Well, he gave me some contact details for help centres which deal with such matters. But, you know, I can't. Here I can talk to you all, I can open up and it makes me feel better, but I just can't talk to others about it. I am so ashamed, I feel I have let myself down. I have shown myself to be weak, unworthy, and you know what, even incompetent. I should be able to stand up to someone at work, shouldn't I? Where's the problem with that? I just don't have the strength."

"Stop, Tina. We've been through this so many times. It is not your fault. He chose you as his next victim. You have to accept that it probably was not even anything personal that he had against you. He needed a new victim because he had successfully seen the previous one buckle under the pressure. Not you, though. You will fight. Didn't we agree this was what you wanted to do?"

"Yes, Andrew, we did. And I will. I have arranged an appointment with HR at Head Office for Friday. I just hope they can help. And I hope I can stay calm during the meeting." She took a deep breath. "I'm sure we're doing the right thing. I don't want to spoil the whole evening again; you had to put up with me last week. Doesn't anyone have something positive we can talk about today?"

"Well," said Janice after a (very) short while. The group looked slightly taken aback; Janice was normally the one responsible for the negative views and attitudes, and here she was (almost) stating something positive. They waited.

"Tim has asked me to marry him."

Wow! Now here we have something positive to celebrate. Everyone beamed – except Janice. The others picked up the vibes and waited for her to explain.

"You have accepted, have you?" asked Tina, trying hard to comprehend Janice`s facial expression.

"He thinks that is what we should do. He thinks it is time. He thinks it is best for Dylan."

"Good grief, Janice," said Lavinia. "Will you pull yourself together! Only you could be so... oh God, I can't even find a word for it. What you are trying to say is, he loves you and wants to marry you, isn`t it? At least, I hope that is what you are trying to say."

"Maybe it is. He did say he loves me – and I am sure he does."

Connor felt it was time to remind Janice. "Have you forgotten how awful you felt when he left you for those few weeks? Have you forgotten how much you wanted him back? How glad you were when he did return?"

"I can remember all of that, and much more. But he doesn`t have to marry me to stay with me, does he? He doesn`t have to marry me to be a good father to our son. And he certainly doesn't have to marry me for me to stay with him. We belong together. That's a given."

Tina had cheered up slightly. "It sounds like good news to me, Janice. You should be thrilled. Wasn't it what you would have wished for only a few weeks ago? The two of you, showing the world that you love each other, that you belong together and wish to spend the rest of your lives together. It's wonderful!"

"How can you be so old-fashioned, Tina?" Janice asked. "Why should we need to play to the world? We have each other and it has always been enough. We have been together for ten years. Why change the parameters now? My guess is, his parents are putting pressure on him. They have probably had enough of our 'open relationship,' as they so often call it. They are the ones who think that we need to change the way we run our lives, I'm sure of it. Tim just would never admit it. So, he harks on about our responsibility towards Dylan and about the fact that nothing else would change other than our legal status. 'Let's do this,' he says, as if it were a house-warming party or something."

Connor was truly saddened to hear Janice talking in such a way. "Janice, I thought you had come to realise that your negative approach to life and your surroundings hindered your happiness. I thought the talks we had were helpful in the sense that you had come to see that you should be more positive in your outlook. And look at you now – instead of being happy at the prospect of marriage, you try to find reasons not to, try to find reasons to keep the status quo, which, if I may say so, is basically a marriage in itself already. You have a son together, you already have legal responsibility. You have been living your lives together for so long, there is responsibility in that as well. What are you afraid of?"

"I'm not afraid."

"I think you are." This prompted nods all round.

Heather stood up; she needed to go to the toilet.

Janice stood up. "My round, the usual for everyone?" Nods all round.

Connor was at a loss to understand. "She should be honest with him, shouldn't she? I don't understand why they don't talk properly to each other. She is completely misunderstanding what he is trying to do. I told her when he left the other month that he had only left in order to force her into action. He wanted to give her a signal that something should change. She managed to act on that, and now she's buggering it up completely. Is not honesty the most important aspect of a relationship?"

Tina agreed wholeheartedly. "Absolutely. She should be thrilled, not looking to find excuses to say no. She loves him, doesn't she? How come they don't just talk directly about it? If it were me in her shoes, I wouldn't hesitate. Seems like a perfectly logical consequence of their life so far that they should marry at some point – and why not now?"

Andrew wanted to partake in the conversation, although he had no real experience in this field. His last real romantic alliance had turned into a disaster and he had been left a disappointed and disillusioned man. He was still trying to overcome his hang-ups in this segment of life. Still, he was trying; he had accepted he was on a learning curve and was trying hard. "Of course, they should marry. But only if they both really want to. Do you think it is true that Tim's parents are behind the idea?" Heather, back at the table, felt it was time to join in the debate.

"The only person who really knows that is Tim, and if he isn't saying... Poor Janice, she can hardly ask outright if that is his motive. We all know what happened last time he decided he had had enough of her negativity. She certainly won't want to go through that again. She was so down when he left. However, she needs to know. Connor is right – honesty is the key to a good marriage and an open relationship needs to be nurtured."

Lavinia agreed, albeit only to a certain extent. "Sometimes it is better not to know everything. Sometimes it is better to let things slide. It is not always a good idea to question everything. But yes, honesty is the key."

As Janice placed the drinks on the table, she heard just the last (semi-) sentence. "Yes, honesty. That is the key. I have to ask him, don't I? There is no way I can start a marriage with him thinking that the only reason we are married at all is because his parents want it like that. I love him. I love our son. I love our life together. I don't need a change. However, if he does, if it really is him that does, we should go for it. Cheers!"

"Here's to Janice and Tim," said Lavinia.

"To their future together," said Andrew.

"To love," said Tina.

"To a positive outcome," said Heather.

"To honesty in relationships," said Connor.

"Cheers!"

Toby stood behind the bar and watched the group from a distance. He smiled an inner smile. It wasn't the revenue they brought in with them; it was more the feeling he got that his pub was a place where people felt cosy and relaxed – his pub as a place of reflection and interaction. How lucky he was.

How lucky Janice was that she should have such a group to talk to. A group that would tell her, straight out, what's what. Put her back on track and allow her to see for herself what's what. There was a refreshing trust element in the set-up.

Part of this luck was that Trish had left. Trish, his wife in name only. Their problem hadn't been a lack of communication. She had always been eager to talk to him, to tell him how lacking he was in just about everything she expected in life.

There were times when he had been glad of a short-term foreign posting, an opportunity to leave her behind and just go away for a few months. There were also times when he had asked himself whether she had secretly hoped he wouldn't come back alive. Was he being too harsh? Probably. But then, it was pretty steep what he had been put through. She had been so dishonest, malevolent, absolutely beastly.

Everyone else seemed to have been aware of her revolving bedroom door; nobody had seen fit to tell him, and he had been too stupid, too naïve to see the writing on the wall. Shit, it was awful once he found out. Found out that not only was she being unfaithful but that everyone else as well had been keeping their mouths shut. It was time to put an end to this. Draw a line under a sorry state of affairs. What a pun! It was time to stop the blamestorming – she was still claiming it was all his fault – and time to cut the losses. He'd kept his powder dry till now, but God help him, he was finished with her now.

2/FIVE

Meanwhile, at home in the suburbs

Positive outcome, indeed, thought Heather as she walked to the Park Lane car park where she had parked her car earlier. She walked slowly; she was in no hurry to get home. *She had just wanted to nip to the toilet and look what happened*, she thought.

How come she had been so blind? There is no such thing as coincidence, this was pure fate playing into her hands. On her way back from the toilet this evening, she had overheard Cath, the barmaid, talking on her phone. She was talking in a whisper, obviously planning some clandestine meeting for tomorrow. She was flustered when she saw Heather, like a child caught with her hand in the sweets' jar, then broke off the call very quickly, just long enough to bid farewell to "Jack," my love. She gazed back in horror at Heather, who had been watching her, and listening. She hurried off to the restaurant bar.

So that was the reason. Heather could see it all now quite clearly. Everything was fine at home because it was all just a façade anyway. A façade to keep Emily happy and her in the dark. How could he do that to her, to them? She felt she was in shock. Never, ever would she have thought he would do such a thing. Such deceit. So much for all this "honesty in relationships" which had dominated the group's talk this evening. He had changed when he started to do his "creative writing" course in evening classes but he had explained that to her. He had said he had been contemplating it for a while, and when she started with her cookery class, he thought it was a good time for him to start his course as well. Seemed plausible enough at the time. Still seemed plausible now, in fact. It was the beginning of a new phase for them. They had become closer due to the fact that they had found an outside interest, outside of their own little world that had, until then, been so engrossing. Even their attitude towards their daughter, Emily, had changed. They were more open towards her. She, too, was beginning to go out and spend more time with friends from school. Indeed, they had undergone quite a little revolution.

And now this!

She had reached the car park, found her car, unlocked it, sat down behind the steering wheel, and was ready to drive home. No, she was ready to drive, but she wasn't ready to drive home. How could she possibly face him?

Should she question him? Should she challenge him? She felt she had to know.

Then she realised that if she questioned him, she would have to question herself – or worse still, maybe he would. Maybe he had known.

She truly regretted starting the affair with Eamon, her boss. It had been a spur-of-the-moment thing; neither had planned it – or so she believed. It had lasted a few weeks, no let's say a while, but then both realised it was not good for either of them. Having an affair with the person you work for is never easy; in fact, it's just as difficult as having an affair with someone who works for you. They had both underestimated the implications. Wrong again, Heather thought; they hadn't considered the implications at all. They had simply started an affair, enjoyed it, discovered the issues it brought along with it, and finished it. They continued to work together as before; they were sure no one had ever noticed, and no one noticed a difference now.

Truth be known, she did still have feelings for him and often yearned for his embrace. Stop, Heather, this is getting you nowhere, she thought. But then she remembered, sometimes in discussions she may still touch his arm slightly to enforce a statement or an interpretation of a situation on him, but basically, she kept a distance. There was a lot of work at the surgery, plenty to keep her busy and out of harm's way. She didn't regret that the affair was over. Really, she didn't.

She was sure her husband, Jack, had never noticed anything. He had never said anything or changed his attitude towards her. No, he didn't know.

She couldn't drive home just yet. She had to be clear in her mind first. What should she do? What a stupid question, she thought. The question is not what should I do; it is what will I do? I have to decide this for myself – what do I want?

Is it so important to know about Jack's affair? Will it help me? Will it help us?

I had an affair. It dawned on Heather that it was extremely difficult to actually articulate such a sentence. How much more difficult would it be if she were to tell Jack? Would he even want to know? Does he need to know?

But then, if I keep quiet about my affair, surely I can't confront him with his. Oh my God – what a mess. This was so obviously something which she would not be able to solve in five seconds in the car park in Park Lane that evening.

That much was abundantly clear, so home she went.

The following days proved very exhausting. Every free moment she spent pondering this aspect of her life. She found no answer, her thoughts just went round and round.

Then she hit on an inspiration: she had to separate the two things completely. Her affair was one thing. It had been a mistake, after all and she regretted it wholeheartedly.

Jack's was another thing all together. He was being unfaithful to her, deceitful, and so hurtful. She felt she needed to know what was behind it and how important the woman was to him.

She pondered and pondered and came up with: first, she had to decide how honest she wanted to be with Jack about her relationship with Eamon. In her mind, it had already become a relationship and was no longer an affair – big difference.

Surely then all else would fall into place.

Easier said than done.

2/SIX

Heather's honesty

Toby had asked Jack to put the "reserved" card on the large table in the bay window. It was Wednesday and the Six Pack would be in later, so although he wouldn´t be there to see them this evening, he wanted to be sure that all went as usual. Sadie and Cath were coming in early and would manage the bar between them. He wasn`t sure how long this was going to take. He had arranged a meeting with his ex-wife, Trish, as it was time to get things sorted. He didn`t want her back; he was certain of that, and he had heard she was planning to live abroad anyway. The time had come to settle all loose ends as far as their relationship was concerned. He headed off with a skip in his pace, but a heavily pounding heart in his chest. This would probably not run as smoothly as he planned; nothing ever did with Trish.

If Toby had been on bar duty, he would have sensed it, but Sadie didn`t know that it was unusual for Janice not only to arrive first, but to arrive on her own. She greeted the woman with a friendly smile and waited for her order. Janice wanted some bubbly. What did they have on offer? Sadie had to check herself; it wasn`t often that they served such a beverage in this bar. No matter, Janice was already walking over to the bay window. Then, as an after-thought, she called out to the barmaid.

"We`ll need six glasses, please. I`ll give you a sign when you can bring them over, okay?"

"You´re on," said Sadie, with a smile.

Connor opened the door and walked in. He didn`t even notice Janice until he was at the table, so engrossed was he in his thoughts, but also so sure that he would be the first to arrive. He always was, well, always had been.

Next in were Tina and Andrew, who had obviously travelled or walked here together. They were deep in conversation, seemingly wanting to clarify something before joining the group. They stopped abruptly once in earshot of the table.

Lavinia and Heather walked in at the same time, though not together. Sadie, at 19, wasn't as experienced behind the bar as Toby and Cath were, but even she could sense something amiss. Lavinia was merry and somehow care-free, while Heather, on the other hand, was extremely pensive and almost distant. They didn't fit. As they sat down next to each other, Janice stood up, waved to Sadie to signal her entrance with the bubbly, and said:

"My round and I have allowed myself to order for all of you. We have something to celebrate and we're going to do it in style!"

"Cheers!"

"You can't leave us in ignorance, Jan. Have you seen the light, or what?" asked Lavinia as she took a second sip.

"I knew after last week's meeting that I really did want to marry Tim, but I was simply afraid he was only asking me because his parents expected it. And that, I didn't want. So, plain and simple solution: I asked him what his parents thought about the idea. And, do you know what? He said he hadn't told them yet. We should go over at the weekend and make the announcement, if I had made up my mind by then. I couldn't believe it! Well, I made up my mind, there and then. I suggested they come over to us, it would be better. So, they came on Saturday evening and after dessert, we told them. They were stunned. They really had no idea. Then, his father said he wanted to talk to Tim in private. They walked off to the study, leaving me with the mother-in-law, wasn't easy, I can tell you that. She didn't say a word the whole time they were away. When they came back to the dining room, a distinct aura of tension arrived with them. To cut a long story short, they left about 10 minutes later. Tim said his father had proclaimed that if he married me, they would not leave their estate to him – they would not have me benefitting from their hard work. He was having no discussion about it. He should think again. Leave things as they were; support Dylan, live with the woman, if necessary, but nothing too formally serious."

Unbelievable! Every single one of the Six Pack were thinking it, but no-one said it. Janice continued:

"So, Tim told him he wasn't going to change his mind. Either they accepted it or not. No hassle. They had until the wedding day to decide how they felt. If they came to the wedding, there was scope for a future relationship, if they didn't, there wasn't." (Janice took a large swig of bubbly). "I was so proud of my Tim. He is my Tim. We belong together, and we will stay together. I am so happy. We've set the date. No turning back now! How come I didn't see this before? I am impossible, aren't I?"

Every single one of the Six Pack thought, well yes, you are to a certain extent, but no one said anything – except "Cheers."

Drunk in the fashion that it had been by this group, the bottle of bubbly didn't last long. Connor knew it was actually his turn to buy a round, so he stood up and asked for the orders: two pints of bitter, one white wine, one gin and tonic, one lager and lime, and one lemonade and lime. Things were back to normal. Off he trotted to the bar with the order. By the time he returned, Tina was in full swing. She was explaining how things were playing out for her at the bank:

"they called on Monday to let me know. I couldn't believe it." She shook her head to underline her statement. "Such a short time and already things are moving. Who would have thought this could change so quickly?"

Connor was alarmed. "How could you start without me, Tina? I've missed the best bit already, have I?"

"No – well, yes. Actually, you have. But it is so brilliant, I'll tell it again, and again, and again if necessary. You remember, I had an appointment at HR? Well, Andrew and I prepared a list of all the things that had happened to me, a really detailed list: days, times, incidents – even ones which, at the time they happened, I hadn't seen in context. It was actually quite a long list once it was finished. The HR group listened intensely. It was a group – there were three of them. That situation had quite daunted me at first, but then I realised that they really were taking this very seriously. Word had got around that something was amiss in the branch. They really did want to get to the bottom of it. They asked all sorts of questions and seemed to almost know what the answers would be.

They even asked me about Stella – you remember? That's the colleague who left a few weeks ago to work in Cornwall. That got me thinking. Anyway, I called her parents when I got home and asked them to give me her telephone number. They were so hesitant, distant, and for a moment, I even thought they would put the phone down on me. They said they would tell her I had called and would give her my number. She called me on Sunday morning – she was in town visiting her parents, so we met up. It was an eye-opener, I can tell you. She was shocked to hear I was on sick leave, especially for the reason I gave her. She opened up and let everything out. Everything she had held back. She had been bullied, too. We agreed that she should talk to HR, just as I had. She just wanted me to promise to apply for a transfer first. Then we would start our attack. From a distance, so to speak."

Tina took a sip of her lager and lime and continued with her narrative: "My sick leave finishes tomorrow. I wasn't looking forward to going back at all. Anyway, on Monday, I got a call from HQ. The HR department wanted to inform me that I was expected back at work. Then came the hammer – they said they had discussed my issues – that's what they called them, "my issues" – and had come to the conclusion that I did have a case. It all sounded so formal, somehow even unreal. They were talking about my feelings, my unease at work as if it were a personnel file case. But then, I suppose it is for them. Well, it seems that in the light of certain irregularities which they had found in the CV of my boss, he is being summoned to HQ for meetings on Thursday and Friday. I am to get a call on Friday to inform me of any further developments in my "case." At the moment, I just feel relieved that something is developing at all. Andrew thinks this is all going my way.

I'm not so sure, but at least I don't have to face the boss for the next two days. And then, I can still apply for a transfer on Monday, can't I?"

Connor held up his beer glass. "I am very proud of you, Tina. You are being very brave."

"I couldn't have done it without Andrew; in fact, I couldn't have done it without you lot. I needed to talk to someone about what was happening. I had no idea it was, in fact, bullying. It never dawned on me that it was. Only talking to you lot made me see it. But you know what? It is so difficult. This feeling of being weak, too weak to stand up to the pressure of the bully. In fact, even using the word, bully, is hard. To have to admit to have been bullied, is quite humiliating, you know."

Lavinia smiled at Tina. She couldn't find the right words, somehow, they just avoided her. She cocked her head and made a face that showed how she felt. "Here's to you, Tina. You're on the right track."

Janice chimed in, "Talking, that's the key, you know. I've learnt that, too. Talk about your feelings, tell people what you think. It is a sign of strength, you know, not weakness. It just takes quite some doing to pull yourself together and actually do it. Cheers, Tina."

Heather stood up. "Unusual as it is, I think we need a third round today. My turn, the usual for everyone?"

Everyone nodded, and off Heather went to the bar. When she returned with the tray of drinks, the group were talking about the council's idea of turning the inner city circle into a pedestrian area. They all thanked her for their respective drink and were surprised that she didn't sit down again. She just stood there, as if waiting for some apparition.

"Something wrong?" asked Andrew

"No, no," answered Heather and sat down. "It's just that...." (There was a pause, much too long for it to be part of a performance, it was a real-life struggle. "all this talk about talking to each other has me thinking. Actually, it was Connor's toast last week, 'To honesty in relationships,' that gave me the kick-start. You see, I have this friend who had an affair with her boss. It is over now, but she worries about the dishonesty towards her husband. He doesn't know about the affair, never noticed anything. She has a bad conscience and feels she should talk to her husband. When she asked me if I thought she should tell him, I said she shouldn't. If she could forget it, then why shake things up unnecessarily? Now, with all this talk about exchanging opinions and feelings, and about honesty, I'm not so sure if I gave her the right answer."

Lavinia was quick to give her opinion on the matter. "I think she should definitely tell him. Obviously, something was amiss, or it would never have happened, would it? If you want to clear the air, then everything has to come out in the open, doesn't it? Believe me, I've been there many times – oh no, not having an affair – I mean clearing the air. I used to let things just run along, brushed aside what I didn't like or didn't agree with, but I wasn't happy like that. Sometimes, you have to rebel a little in order to show your discontent. Life is a lot more rosy then. Maybe that is what she was doing. Simply playing the rebel a little to make things better in the long run. But then, what's the use of that if she doesn't tell him? They definitely have to talk."

Janice was slightly less forceful but agreed. "Yes, I think they need to talk about it, too. If Tim had started an affair while we were separated for those few weeks, then I would want to know. I would have to know in order to press the re-start button. How can you have a re-start if one of the partners doesn't know it is a re-start? It would have changed things, I guess, but I would have wanted to know."

Andrew couldn't follow this line of thought: "What about if you had started an affair during the break-up? That is the question here, isn't it? Would you have told him about it? I mean, you had broken up. You were no longer in a relationship, so basically, all would have been in order, but would you have said anything?"

Janice looked down at the floor. "I think not. I wouldn't have been sure how he would react. I wouldn't have risked it if I thought he was returning."

"Well, enough said then, really, don't you think?"

Tina wasn't in a romantic relationship, so she didn't know if she had any right to join in, but she did have strong feelings about such matters. "I strongly believe that if a relationship is to work, then the two people involved need to be honest. Respectful, but honest. So, what I'm saying is, she should talk to her husband, but she should be very careful how she says things. Her words will all be weighed up with an intensity that was maybe never there before."

Andrew didn't agree. "Oh, Tina. Why rock the boat? If he doesn't know, why not leave it like that? Maybe he does know, but doesn't want to talk about it. Maybe he knew all along but was afraid to talk about it, afraid of the consequences. Afraid of the result, afraid of the decision he may feel he is being forced to make. If he hasn't said anything, and she feels that all is well again, I think she should leave it."

"Is that what you would do if the shoe was on the other foot?" Tina wanted to know.

Andrew felt like he was being misunderstood. "I'm not saying I would act like that, for the simple reason I don't think I would cheat on my partner and I would assume the same for her."

"Purely hypothetical all of this, then," said Connor with a rather smug sort of look on his face. Heather nodded. So, he continued, "Surely, it would depend on what kind of a husband your friend has. I mean, if he were a jealous type, things could get tricky. He could start to question the relationship. Not too rosy an outlook. If he were the understanding type, he could accept it as a past thing and forget about it. She would run the risk of it flaring up at every heated discussion in the future, though. Not too grand an outlook, either. Then again, it would depend on what kind of a relationship the two of them had before it happened. If all had been running smoothly and everyone seemed happy enough, then one could pass the whole thing off as a mishap. A one-off shitty mistake. But then we come back to the type of man the husband is, don't we? Bottom line for me is, if it is really over, as your friend is claiming, and she is sure it can't be rekindled, then I'd say, let bygones be bygones."

"Your idea of honesty in relationships is very short-lived, Connor. It only seems to be alive as long as no-one really puts it to the test." Janice had found her voice again.

"I'd say it is alive as long as no-one is in danger of being hurt. Do you realise how long it would take to re-build the trust lost? How hurtful the whole episode could be to the other person involved? That is a high price to pay for a simple mad moment, don't you think?"

Heather had become very pensive. "Connor, you mentioned trust. Surely, trust needs to be based on honesty, doesn't it? What if the husband, by some quirk of fate, found out at some point in the future? Wouldn't that really put the trust between them to an immense test?"

"Of course it would. At work, at the hospice, we often have people who want to ease their conscience before they die. They don't think about what effect their confession is going to have on their families. They want to go with a clean slate, and fortunately, many stick to confessing to someone outside the family. This is only slightly different. She wants a clean slate, but here, the difference would be she has to continue to live her life. So, in my view, if the whole thing is squarely a thing of the past, the lover has disappeared – or at least is no longer in the immediate surroundings, the marriage back on cloud nine, and there is no possibility of any renewal of the affair, then all would turn out okay. You were right to tell her to let it go."

"And if one of those criteria you just mentioned were not the case, then I was wrong."

"That's how I would see it. But, at the end of the day, your dear friend has to decide herself. She knows all the facts, she knows all the characters, and she knows the current state of affairs much better than you do. She knows whether she is considering talking to him in order to clear her conscience, or if she really wants to discuss the matter. Is she willing to admit her own guilt, or is she going to plant some guilt on him? Maybe she thinks it was his fault she went looking for someone else?"

"No, no, she certainly didn't go looking. It just happened," she spurted it out rather too quickly.

Everyone around the table looked at each other. *Okay*, they all thought. *Message understood.*

"May the force be with you. Drink up!" said Connor.

The Six Pack left the pub slightly later than usual and Sadie was already cleaning and tidying up as they walked out the door. She couldn`t help but overhear pieces of their conversation during the evening. They were a little louder than normal after the round of bubbly. And somehow, the eyes, and ears had followed over to the group after Connor (that`s what he said his name was) had bought the next round of drinks for them all.

I`m sure that Janice works at the bank, so the boss she was talking about can only be that Simon bloke from the tennis club.

She`d already heard some nasty rumours about him, behind the bar you hear so much, and one day he actually came in to the restaurant for lunch. Cath said he was detestable, had deplorable manners and was a sexist to the core. *Tennis club*, she thought, *Vicky works there at the weekends.* She made a mental note to ask Vicky what he was like at the club. Her bet was he was an arsehole there as well. *You wait*, she thought, *this town isn`t as big as you think. If you are mucking up people`s lives, you are in for a shock.* She didn`t dwell on thoughts of either Simon, or Vicky for long. She had other things going through her mind. Just how understanding and kind that Connor had been. *There are men like that still around*, she thought. She hadn`t had too much luck in her choice of boyfriend to-date, she had become convinced she had been looking for the wrong type and concentrating on the wrong values.

Here, tonight, she had seen (and heard) some other qualities, which, from her present perspective, were well, interesting.

2/SEVEN

Meanwhile, at the tennis club

Sadie worked at the pub five days a week. In theory, she had Mondays and Tuesdays off; in practice, this varied. This week, for example, she had worked on Tuesday as Cath wanted the day off, so she was free on Thursday. She had decided to use the day off to gather some info about "Slippery Simon," as she now called him. It wasn't really that she was particularly interested in Simon or his bullying, or whether he was macho or not, but she thought that very probably, with certain snippets of info, she could possibly wiggle herself into a position where Connor would take notice of her. She found herself quite smitten with him. Could hardly think of anything else. This seemed like an opportunity too good to miss.

Off she headed to the tennis club on the pretence of wishing to catch up with her old school friend, Vicky. The tennis club offered snacks at lunchtime. She would have lunch there and grab her moment when Vicky was on a break. The place was almost empty when she arrived, so she had a choice of tables; she picked one in good view of the bar. She placed her jacket on the chair, walked over to the bar, and ordered a cider and a round of ham and cheese sandwiches. It wasn't Vicky who served her, so she asked where Vicky was - on a break, and would be back shortly. That was a relief; for a moment, she thought she had been too quick to order everything if Vicky wasn't even here today. She took her glass of cider and walked back to the table, only to see Simon, the very Simon she wanted to talk about, walking towards the clubhouse. This she hadn't foreseen, hadn't considered it an option for a moment. Hadn't Tina said he had been summoned to HQ?

He walked straight past her, not a sign of recognition, and not a sign of pleasantness, either. But then came Vicky. She walked straight past him, with a definite sign of recognition and an unmissable sign of vindictiveness. He just smiled as if nothing were amiss.

Vicky managed a smile for Sadie but said, "I loathe that man!" Things were looking up for Sadie. She hadn't thought it would be this easy.

Vicky was glad to have someone she could open up to here and now. She had known Sadie for years. They had started school together and had been friends throughout. Only that once, when she had inadvertently blurted out something Vicky had told her in confidence, had they had an almighty row and had avoided each other like the plague… But Vicky had forgiven her after a while, and all was well again.

Vicky told Sadie all about Simon and his advances. He was the devil in disguise as far as she was concerned. Not only did he have his hands everywhere, he bragged about all his encounters and was an absolute cheat. He simply made up stories if he thought he needed to be the centre of attention and lied when cornered. Definitely, a man to be avoided at all costs. She wondered how his wife dealt with it. She was such a nice woman. Always friendly, chatty and certainly not the type which you would think would fall for such a two-faced bugger. Then she said, "Last week, he grabbed me in the locker room. Wouldn't take no for an answer. God knows what would have happened if some members hadn't arrived to get ready for their training. I don't think he would have gone too far, much too risky in that scenario, but it was awfully frightening. I wouldn't like to meet him in a dark alley."

Sadie couldn't believe her luck. Did she have something for Connor? Well, actually, for Tina. This must help Tina's case, surely. Should she drop by the hospice and tell him? No, that really would be pushing it, wouldn't it? Tempting though it was, she thought she should maybe wait with this info – especially as Vicky had made her promise not to say a word to anyone.

Vicky had proclaimed, forewarned is forearmed. She didn't intend to get in any way involved with that man. She would steer really clear of him from now on. For her, and with that, the case was closed.

She was very curious to know how Sadie was faring on the boyfriend front. Sadie wasn't sure she should say anything about Connor just yet.

It was much too early for that, but she did say that she had a crush on a bloke she had seen at the pub and felt strangely attracted to him even though she hardly knew him. Vicky pushed for more, but got nowhere. That made her realise, this could be something serious.

She let it go, not because she wanted to, but because a group had arrived at the bar, and she had to get back to work. By the time she had finished serving their drinks and getting their snack lunches, Sadie had gone. Without saying goodbye.

2/EIGHT

Andrew's Ambitions

It was Wednesday, and at 5:30, Toby placed the "reserved" card on the round table in the bay window. Such a pity he missed last week's session of the group. Sadie had told him they drank bubbly for starters. He had wondered what they were celebrating, but no problem; he found out soon enough. When Tim came in with his group, he was telling everyone who wanted to know, and even those who didn't, that he and Janice were going to get married – and soon. Toby was happy for them; they were a nice couple. He walked back to the bar as a few regulars from 'Sherman's, the Insurance People' walked in for their after-work pint.

Connor arrived over-punctually, as always. He sat down and stared out of the window, recalling all that Heather had said last week. It all fitted so well into what she had told him during their cookery classes. She felt smothered, almost too loved at home. Felt she had no space for herself, no freedom. I bet she was the woman with the conscience. He had actually heard rumours of Dr Brewer (Heather's boss) being romantically-linked to a married woman. Yes, that's how the women at work had phrased it. They were such gossips, you couldn't get away from it however hard you tried. Well, maybe it was indeed that he knew who the mystery woman was. How's that for coincidence?

"Hi, Connor," he heard from across the floor. Andrew had turned up. This didn't happen often – the two men sat on their own. It didn't last long either, Andrew's bottom had hardly hit the seat before Lavinia and Janice walked in. They sat down after hanging their coats on the hooks on the wall to the left of Connor.

Tina was next. "I just saw Heather coming along the road, she'll be here in a minute." She was.

It was Andrew's round. "I'll get the drinks," he said before the last two to arrive had even settled in their chairs. He didn't ask what they wanted, he just went up to the bar and ordered.

"I'd have bought bubbly if I had the cash, but I guess drinking what we all enjoy is fine, too, isn't it?" he said as he placed the tray of drinks on the table.

"You have something to celebrate, then?" asked Lavinia. Tina looked surprised, no, more than surprised, she looked astonished. How come she didn't know anything about this?

"Indeed I do. I have been offered a contract at the DIY store. Full contract, assistant manager. Training on the job, starting on the first of next month," he smiled.

"Congratulations!" they were all sincerely pleased he was finally getting somewhere job-wise.

"Not what I had foreseen for myself, but I suppose everyone has to start somewhere, don't they?"

Tina noticed his hesitance. "It gives you some stability, financially as well as socially. Why aren't you happier?"

"I am happy for myself. It's just the circumstances that surround the offer are not kosher. At least not from where I am standing."

"What on earth do you mean?" It was Janice who asked, although the faces showed that all around the table the same question was sounding.

"The manager called me into his office this morning. He said they had been watching how I worked and sensed that I was reliable, stable, hard-working, with an eye for the overview. The current assistant manager is leaving to work for some oil company, and he would like to offer me the job. Would I take it? I was quite stunned really, it was so out of the blue. I had no idea Dan was thinking of leaving, but I guess with his wife pregnant again, he was looking for more money. Anyway, he gave me the details and said he'd have the contract made up for me by tomorrow morning."

"Sounds reasonably believable to me. Where are you smelling a fish?"

"I think he wants someone who will be at his beck and call and will do what he says. If he says jump, I should only ask how high. Don't you see? Why else would he offer me the job? There are plenty of others around. Some already on full contracts, some who have been there much longer than I have. Even some of the other zero-hour workers have been at the place longer. Surely they should be asked first. It just doesn't seem right. Why me?"

Lavinia knew the answer to this question. "Because you are a British, white male, that's why."

Heather added, "A British, white male with a degree."

"In oceanology, may I remind you. That won't help me much selling paints and wood now, will it?"

Tina felt it was time to step in. "Why are you doing this to yourself, Andrew? You know you have it in you. You can do it. The manager has seen it too. Why on earth are you questioning his choice?"

Connor intervened. "I get his point. He thinks his manager thinks he's a push-over and believes he'll accept because he has no better choice at present. Andrew, you just have to show him your trueself. Prove to him you're not what he believes you to be. It shouldn't take long."

Andrew knew it was time to present the real problem. "I don't want to be an assistant manager of a DIY store. I don't even want to be a manager of a DIY store. That is not what I studied for. It is not my aim in life. There must be something better out there for me. It is not that I think I can't handle it – or the manager – it's that I want to have more. I am just waiting for the right job to come along."

"How many applications have you sent out in the last few weeks?" asked Janice.

"Around 40, I think."

"And how many interviews have you had?"

"Two – what are you trying to say? That I shouldn't wait for anything better because I won't find it, or if I find it, I won't get the job anyway?"

"Hold your horses, matey." Janice didn't like the road this was taking. "What I'm saying is that you should take the job, learn the ropes, and make the money. Alongside applying for that perfect job that you hope is awaiting you around the corner."

"Doesn't that seem unfair to the others who should have had the job offered to them? I'm only filling time, I'll be gone as soon as something better crops up. There are others who would love this opportunity and deserve it as well. I don't."

Tina felt anger creeping up through her body but suppressed it to an extent. He had been there for her when she needed to be pushed in the right direction; now it was her turn to help him. "You bloody well do deserve it. You have worked for them, you have been loyal, you have been reliable, and they want you to stay. They want to give you this opportunity. Take it, for Christ's sake. Stop thinking about others. They have to care for themselves. Do you think for one second that they would hesitate to accept such an offer just because they thought (any of them, that is) that you (or anyone else, for that matter) could actually do the job better? They wouldn't, believe you me."

Lavinia, although she liked Andrew and wished him well, needed to remind everyone of the real issue here. "Listen, Mr British, white male, I get your point. I, too, see a certain amount of discrimination in this whole set-up. Help me here, how many of the colleagues who you think could do the job are women?"

"Well, four actually. But two of them are Polish, so I don't know if they would be accepted on a management course."

"Hold up here," said Heather. "Discrimination on the grounds of nationality is just as bad as discrimination on the grounds of gender. Are you honestly saying the company doesn't send foreign nationals on training courses?"

"Heck, I don't know, do I? I've been on a zero-hour contract until now. I have no idea of the company policy on anything, really. I'm just saying how I feel at the moment. Don't put words into my mouth."

Lavinia was not going to be waylaid. "How many women do they have on the staff, in percentage?"

Connor was quick off the mark. "It's a DIY store, Lavinia. Be fair, it would be only too normal to have more men than women, wouldn't it? Talk about barking up the wrong tree."

"Look, I think, Andrew, there are plenty of women who do DIY, and some who do it better than men. I wouldn't have any problem asking a woman for help, or advice when it comes to DIY. Okay, I will admit that in the warehouse where physical strength is needed, then maybe men are better positioned, but other than that..."

"Listen, Lavinia," Andrew had heard enough. "My point was that I thought I shouldn't be given the job because maybe someone else was more in line for it. I said nothing about whether it should be a man or a woman. How come you women always find a way to turn things into some kind of gender struggle? Just leave it, will you? Men face discrimination, as well, you know."

"Not half as much as we women do! I'll not have you turning me into a radical feminist just because I think that women should be given equal rights."

"At the hospice, I work with a load of women, and do you know what, they have a struggle amongst themselves. Sometimes, they wouldn't give each other the time of day, and then, oh wonder, if they are attacked from the outside – i.e. by a man – they gang up and suddenly become a force. There is way too much talk of women being discriminated against, always forming everything into a potential gender fight."

Heather thought Lavinia needed some back-up. "Hey, guys, just look at the past and you may begin to understand why women feel they need to fight for their rights and assert their positions. For too long, we have been left out of the loop. It is time to ensure equality. Wage-wise, we have a long path to wade along, but when it comes to labour rights, we should not have to encounter stones every step of the way, should we?"

Janice knew what the woman meant. "Never a truer word said. We are constantly having to prove ourselves, you know what they say, women have to prove they are competent, men have to prove they are incompetent. Fits just almost always. Tell us, Andrew, so we put this back into perspective, were the four women you mentioned on your list of people who maybe could do the job better than you?"

Tina wanted this over with, so she rushed to the rescue. "Hold on. Andrew can do the job and he can do it well. It is purely his sense of social justice that even tempted him to look at the situation in the way he did. No-one should turn it into a gender race, or fight, or whatever. He didn't have to question the offer, did he?"

"Okay, okay, maybe I overstepped the mark. My round… same as always?"

The group nodded, and off she went to the bar to get the drinks.

Tina was pleased for Andrew. She smiled at him with a warmth that could almost be felt around the table. "Andrew, you are going to accept, aren't you?"

"I guess so. I have to move out of the flat soon. My uni-mate is coming back, he's already warned me I have to leave when he arrives. It's just not big enough for the two of us. That alone would be reason enough to have a full contract under my belt. I don't have much choice really, do I? Anyway, I guess it's more than just coincidence that this has happened now. I shouldn't look this gift horse in the mouth. Silly even to think twice about it, really."

Lavinia returned with the drinks and set the tray down on the table.

Janice asked Tina, "Did that info I sent you help in any way regarding your boss?"

"Oh yes, thank you so much. I meant to thank you last week but completely forgot."

"And how are things going?"

"Well" she paused. It was a very dramatic pause. "He didn`t come in to work on Monday or yesterday," (another pause) "and this morning we were informed by HQ that he has been suspended. Rumour has it that the "irregularities" on his CV, which HR mentioned to me were quite profound and when followed up, led to his dismissal. All rumours at the moment, but one thing is sure, he is not coming back to our branch. How`s that for good news? The tables have really turned."

"Cheers!" – could be heard well beyond the bay window.

Toby had had extra help this evening at the bar. For some reason, Sadie had actually volunteered to come over from the restaurant. All the same to me, he had thought. Actually he rather preferred to have Sadie here, rather than Cath. Cath could be quite a difficult character at times, and hand on heart, he didn`t really trust her. He thought maybe she was spying on him for Trish and passing on info. Let her look, his slate was clean. She was acting rather strange recently, though.

He had been quite amused at the group`s conversation today. He, too, thought that women made much too much of a song-and-dance about this equality business. He was the first to admit that if they did the same job, then they should get the same salary, but hand-on-heart, did they ever really do the same job – to the same extent? Wasn`t it always the women who wanted equality until something happened and they needed to have some kind of extra treatment? We have to understand if the time of the month has come – before and after – we have to understand if their children are sick, we have to understand he had to force himself to stop this line of thought.

He was being unfair to women, and he knew it. He couldn`t help himself. But they were unfair to men too, weren`t they? What on earth was wrong with the old idea that there were certain things a man could do better, and certain things a woman could do better? Where did we take a wrong turn? If we all stuck to what we can do best and leave everyone else to do the same, surely we would all be better off. Men have problems, too, you know. He thought. Not least financial ones. Off track again. What was wrong with him?

He was pleased Andrew had been offered a full-contract. He liked the lad. He was always friendly, polite, in no way aggressive, simply a pleasant character. He'll be taken advantage of soon enough. But for now, it did look as though he was going to take up the offer of a job. That could come in handy, having a regular working at the DIY store.

He was even more pleased that things were working out for Tina. You see, he said to himself smugly, no need to fret, things sort themselves out in the end. No need to get involved in other people's issues.

Plenty of his own to worry about – and who, in God's name, was going to help him?

2/NINE

Meanwhile, at the DIY store

Andrew hadn't slept well. He had tossed and turned well beyond three this morning and had then fallen into an uneasy doze. He called it a doze even though it had lasted three hours because it certainly wasn't anything near what one could call "sleep."

He tried showering and shaving as he thought this might make him look a little more presentable, but it didn't. He arrived at work at 8.30 am for a shift which started at 10 am, looking bedraggled and bleary-eyed but determined to sort things out. He headed for William's office on the first floor. Knocked on the door and entered.

William smiled at him; he had expected him to be in later, but this was fine with him. He had the contract ready for him to sign on his desk in front of him.

Andrew sat down and took a deep breath. William felt first signs of unease, maybe this wasn't going to go quite how he thought. No, he couldn't imagine that. Andrew must be over the moon at the offer he had made him. There was just no way he wouldn't accept. He said nothing and waited for Andrew to say something. Andrew didn't. He just sat there, obviously struggling to find the right words. Then, he started.

Andrew had considered the offer made to him and was greatly appreciative of the opportunity (William looked intrigued). It was much more than he had expected after such a short stint (William now slightly less worried). He would very much like to accept (William smiled), but he felt he had to be honest with the company (William nodded, and waited)

After a further deep breath, Andrew laid out his idea of how they could tackle the fact that he would love to take on a full contract but wished to ensure the company didn't expect him to stay here for any length of time because of the opportunity they were giving him. He needed to know that, should an opening arise for him in an area closer to his heart (oceanology, or any affiliated field), he could get up and go, at short notice and without any restrictions, obligations, or hard feelings.

William assured him there were no strings attached to the training scheme and that it was more a hands-on, practice type of training he would be getting. The period of notice was four weeks. He saw no problems ahead. They would not stand in the way of his career in his chosen field if the chance should occur. He pushed the contract over towards Andrew.

However, Andrew wasn't finished with his deliberations. A full contract was a welcome move, no question and he certainly was not about to refuse that. However, he thought it would be a grand idea and benefit all concerned if he took a job-share regarding the assistant manager.

William couldn't believe what he had just heard.

Job-sharing? How on earth should that work here?

Andrew had thought this through (between 12 and 3 am this morning, it had seemed the perfect solution). He would take on a full contract, carry the title of assistant manager, and train on the job. A second person - someone already on a full contract - could do the same, of course. It's a perfect win-win.

No-one on the staff gets their nose poked out of joint, the scheduling for the shifts is easier, and the company is safe in the knowledge that they will not be short of an assistant manager at the drop of a hat.

His enthusiasm for the idea was almost contagious. William was already warming to the idea. He, too, had considered what the news of Andrew's promotion was going to do to the work climate. He wanted to know if Andrew had any thoughts on who is "partner" should be. Andrew did: Sam.

Sam was the perfect choice: competent, long-standing employee, liked by all, trustworthy, reliable, hard-working....

"But she's a woman," said William.

"Exactly," replied Andrew.

It took a while for William to fully comprehend what he had just heard, but once the idea started to grow, the more he warmed to it. Why not, indeed? Yes. Andrew's contract was already approved. Sam was already on full contract. If we offered her training, she would be pleased. Plus, the women would be quiet as one of "theirs" had been given a promotion. Wouldn't cost them a penny more, either. If Andrew was willing to "share" the title with her, what could go wrong? My God, why not, indeed.

"Have you spoken to her about it?"

"No, not yet. I thought that should come from you, don't you think?"

William concurred he would talk to Sam about the suggestion as soon as he had clarified the situation with admin and HQ.

With that, they signed the contract as it stood. Andrew had a job! A full-time, full contract with his name on it.

2/TEN

Lavinia's Lacramae

It was Wednesday, six o'clock in the evening, and there was no "reserved" card on the large round table in the bay window of the Woolpack. Toby had forgotten it. Toby was doing a lot of forgetting these days. Somehow, he was not quite himself. He moped around, forcing a smile when the regulars came in, but avoiding any eye contact, or any real conversation with anyone. Jack was worried, Sadie thought it odd, but not disturbing, and Cath was, as always, happy-go-lucky and hardly noticed a change in anything but her own mirror image.

Connor arrived, greeted Toby and walked over to "their" table. He didn't even notice that the card wasn't there. As he sat down, in came Andrew and Tina, deep in conversation, as always. How strange, he thought, the two of them: a pair but not a pair. They greeted him and Tina sat down opposite him, Andrew then next to her. Janice appeared at the door. She seemed confused and looked around the pub. She was actually looking for Lavinia, who she hadn't met at the supermarket car park, which was normally the case. No matter, she would come eventually. She stood a little too long and obviously slightly in the way at the entrance and was almost shoved out of the way by Heather as she strolled in. Whoops!

As they sat down, Tina stood up. "My round today. Same as always for everyone?" She hadn't considered waiting for Lavinia to arrive. There was no question of her coming. They always met – every Wednesday. Off she went to the bar and ordered the drinks. It was Sadie who served her. Toby had disappeared into the back of the pub.

As she carried the drinks tray back to the table, she was surprised that Lavinia still had not arrived. *Hope she comes*, she thought, *her drink is the most expensive one.*

"Cheers!"

"Okay," said Connor. "I have news for Heather. Want to hear it?" he had a grin from one ear to the other, which made Heather (and the others) particularly interested in what he was about to convey. "My ladies at the hospice tell me – well, actually not me, but anyone who wishes to listen, that you are leaving the surgery. Word has it that you will be gone by the end of next month."

"My God, what a town we live in! This just takes the biscuit. I only handed my notice in last Friday."

"So it is true, then. Wow, I thought it was just another of their cock-and-bull stories designed purely to make themselves interesting?"

"No, it is true. I am going to work in Admissions at the hospital. I had been toying with the idea for a while but put it on the back burner, then, I suddenly decided it was time for a change."

"Just like that?" asked Connor as if smelling a rat.

"Yes, Connor, just like that. Don`t try to make any more of it. Time for a change, that`s all."

"Okay, fine with me. Time for a change of criteria. I get it. No problem here. All hunky-dory," he winked at her in the hope that she would understand that he was not going to follow anything up, although he knew what she was doing. She got the message.

"Yes. I am quite looking forward to it. The hours are much better for me and the travel time is considerably less. Not to mention the pay. What can I say; things are looking up. Cheers everyone."

As they all joined in with the toast, Lavinia walked through the door. She hesitated. Swallowed hard, took a deep breath and continued her path towards the Six Pack that she had come to really like.

"Sorry I`m late," she said and battled with the tears forming in her eyes. "Wow, my g and t ready and waiting. You are the best, you lot. Down the hatch." She took a rather too-hasty and rather too-large a sip and placed the glass back on the table. When she looked up, she realised that all eyes were on her. Waiting.

"What's wrong?" she said

"You tell us," said Janice.

"What?"

"Don't beat about the bush, we can handle it, we can take it. What's up?" Andrew was curious.

"My sister–in–law is getting married."

Everyone waited for more info. This alone could not be the reason for Lavinia being so upset.

"She is so spiteful. She is only doing this to make me feel bad, awkward. To prove she is better. She is arranging everything in such a way as to ……..." she couldn't finish. Her emotions took over, and the tears poured out.

"Calm down, now," said Heather. "It can't be that bad. What on earth has made you so upset?"

"For starters, she has set the date for 20th June – next year – she knows that is my birthday. She knows we were planning a big party as it falls on a weekend."

"That's really unfortunate."

"Not unfortunate – planned."

"You don't know that for sure, now, do you?" Heather was in her surgery mode and trying to calm the situation. "Have you spoken to her about the date? Did she know you were planning a big celebration? It is even possible that, for all her joy of the wedding, she has even forgotten it is your birthday."

"Oh, but that is not all. Then she says she wants to have the wedding in the cathedral and the reception at the Manor House Hotel. She is only trying to poke me in the eye with that."

Janice could remember Lavinia`s wedding all those years ago. It was a grand affair, quite the upper-class kind of do, all the girls were jealous. "Lavinia, what are you saying? You begrudge her, wanting to make it a lovely day to remember forever?

Your wedding was lovely, you can`t possibly have forgotten that. Everyone – well, almost everyone (she thought of the plans she and Tim were making) – wants to make it a day to remember."

"You haven`t heard enough? How about this gem … Chelsey`s not a bridesmaid. She has asked her future husband's two nieces. Can you beat that?"

"Now we know for sure, the green-eyed monster strikes." Andrew had had enough of this silly, childish behaviour.

Lavinia stared at Andrew, willing some catastrophe to strike upon him. Men just didn`t get it, did they?

Connor knew all about the weapon of the woman – tears – and wanted to ensure they didn`t get a full attack. He couldn`t understand why she was so terribly upset about this, but was trying hard to find some aspect of the matter that may cause her at least to reconsider her position. "Does Chelsey want to be a bridesmaid?"

"What?"

"Does Chelsey, that`s your daughter, isn`t it? Have you asked her if she wants to be a bridesmaid?"

"I don`t need to. All girls want to be a bridesmaid."

"I never did," blurted Janice

"I never have been a bridesmaid, and I don`t think anything is missing in my life because of it," added Tina

"Well, you're all not normal then," Lavinia had completely lost her countenance now.

Heather thought about her Emily: "I'm not sure that a young girl these days wants to be a bridesmaid at their aunt's wedding. They want to be bridesmaids at the friends' weddings, maybe. That is a completely different kettle of fish. But aunts' and uncles', no way."

"So, you haven't checked with Chelsey, then. Lavinia, that has to be your first port of call on this. You should talk to her first. You shouldn't attack your sister-in-law until you've gathered your facts."

Janice saw that the glasses were empty. She knew it was her turn to get the round. "My round. Same as always, everyone?" she observed the nods. "Lavinia, could you help me with the glasses, please?"

Lavinia pulled an expression which was somewhere between utter frustration and utter disbelief, but stood up anyway and shrugged her shoulders, "Sure."

They returned to the table a while later with the drinks and with a changed Lavinia. Calm, yes, normal, in fact.

"Cheers," she said. "Okay. You all win. I'll talk to Chelsey. If she's okay with not being a bridesmaid, I'll let it go."

"Good on you, Lavinia," this was Andrew. "And what about the rest of your tribulations? Do they then disappear, too?" He couldn't help himself.

Connor rolled his eyes. "Leave it be, Andrew. Can't you see how much this all means to Lavinia? Give her some time to digest, won't you?"

"I've digested, Connor. I'm okay. If Chelsey is okay with the situation, I'm okay with it, as well. We'll have a ball at the Manor House, and it'll be a classy but boring event. And then, come September, Ian and I will celebrate our wedding anniversary and my birthday with the mother of all knees-ups. We'll show them how to party!"

It was Andrew's turn to roll his eyes. In fact, most of the group did, too. Only Janice didn't. Should she maybe reconsider the wedding she was planning? Was such a reception really so important? Did it really matter how other people saw the event? She'd have to have a think about that and then talk to Tim. She suddenly realised, she hadn't asked him yet what he really felt about their plans so far. He had always just nodded and agreed to what she had suggested.

Toby cleared up the glasses once they had gone.

He had returned to the bar in time to overhear the conversation between Janice and Lavinia as they had got the second round of drinks. He now knew more – a little had he got from Ian when he was in with the lads last week. Lavinia was so upset that their daughter had not been asked to be a bridesmaid. Ian thought it was completely out of perspective to get so irate about it, but heck, that's women for you, he had said. Now Toby had heard the women discussing it. Janice had been quite forceful, yes, she always had been one to put her foot into it by being so damn negative all the time, but here it had worked a treat. Lavinia had a bee in her bonnet, all right. She clearly didn't like Ian's sister and truly resented her getting a better wedding, but the crunch was the bridesmaid. Or that is how she wanted to present it to the world. Actually, as Janice so diplomatically put it – you have a bone to pick with your sister-in-law and are using Chelsey. That is simply not fair to Chelsey. She probably doesn't even want to be bridesmaid and wear some frilly dress and dress up like the other two. Chelsey is a damned independent young woman. If Lavinia were to go on like this, she would have Chelsey to contend with next. It worked.

I'll have my chance, though, Lavinia had warned as she walked away. Toby didn't doubt she would mix some poisoned chalice with her sister-in-law's name on it one day. My God, people who don't have problems have to invent, don't they?

Talking of problems, he too, had heard the rumour of Heather leaving the surgery. It had caused quite a stir. Seems Dr Brewer was taken by surprise and is devastated. Wonder if there is any truth in the old rumour that he had an affair with Heather? Were all women at it?

Couldn't trust them as far as you can throw them. No, not Heather. Her husband, Jack, such a nice guy. But who knows

Toby sat down at the table he was wiping. He had begun to realise that Trish's behaviour towards him had horribly coloured his view of women in general. He no longer trusted any of them. *It was only sex*, she had said the first time he asked her. *You're away so much*, the second time. *I don't feel loved by you any more*, the third time. He had then stopped questioning her, confronting her with his suspicions. Then he realised that it was not only the infidelity. It was lack of respect, not to mention lack of love. Their marriage was over. It wasn't the army's fault. It was their fault, and their fault only.

Now she was claiming it was purely his fault. She had done everything she could to save their marriage. But he was now married to his pub. Just like the army before, he had a partner in life who was not her. She had tried – or so she said – so hard. Her lawyer believed every word that came out of her mouth. She was probably sleeping with him now. *Yes, see – that is how far I have come – can't even think straight.* But how could he when she was about to destroy everything he had?

Can't think straight, I really need a Six Pack, don't I? he thought as he stood up and went back to his bar. Yes, his bar, but for how much longer? He didn't sleep well.

2/ELEVEN

Meanwhile, at the "Pizza Palace"

Lavinia had invited Chelsey out for a pizza dinner. Chelsey hadn`t thought anything of it as her brother was away on a school trip, and her Dad was playing in a tennis tournament. But her mother seemed oddly nervous. She was playing with her wedding ring all the time. Turning it round and round, plus she had flattened her skirt down over her knees at least four times since they sat down at the table in the corner of the restaurant. Whatever, Chelsey had a clear conscience for once, she hadn`t done anything untoward over the last few days, hadn`t even argued with George. Now, that was a feat to be noted. He was such a bore and such a strain on her nerves. Oh, to have a sister, an older sister, would be great, but really, any sister would be better than being burdened with George.

The waitress arrived with the drinks and took their order of pizza. What a funny look Mum has in her eyes, thought Chelsey as she took a sip of her Coke. It didn`t take long to find out what the trouble was. Lavinia couldn`t wait to get it off her chest. She needed to know whether Chelsey would like to be a bridesmaid for her aunt.

There was no need to take her out for a meal to ask that, surely. The answer was simple. No, she didn`t. She had absolutely no craving whatsoever to be dressed up in puff sleeves and pearls and follow her aunt down the aisle. Far from it, if it were up to her, she wouldn`t even go to the wedding, at all. She found her aunt to be snobbish and arrogant. How anyone could want to marry her was a mystery to her. They had never seen eye-to-eye on anything they had talked about. Not that they spoke much, but when they did, it was either completely hollow small talk, or it was something that turned into an argument because she knew better than anyone else what was right and what was wrong. She had even once claimed that Chelsey should feel privileged to be growing up as her niece. No, Mum, the last thing I want is to be a bridesmaid at that woman's wedding.

Lavinia could understand her daughter's feelings. She wasn't particularly fond of her sister-in-law, either. But, this was a chance in a lifetime, didn't she see that?

Chelsey didn't see.

We don't need to have this conversation anyway. She's hardly likely to ask me again, is she? I have already told her I don't want to be her bridesmaid.

Lavinia stared at her daughter. "You never told me that."

"Yes, she asked me when we spoke about the date. She was checking it would be okay for us."

"You never told me that, either."

Chelsey was of the opinion that neither of the conversations had been important enough to waste any precious words on. She didn't see where the trouble lay.

However, there was one thing that she would like to talk to her mother about. She was wondering if she could go to Ben's party in two weeks' time. His parents were away on holiday, but his older brother (much older) was home from university and would make sure everything was above board.

She was sure her mother would remember Ben. He was the "lovely young man" that they had been introduced to at the reception for the town council. His Dad was in politics. They lived in the large house up on Thresher Hill. Surely she wasn't against this friendship, was she?

Lavinia was still in a state of semi-shock. Her disdain for her sister-in-law had increased exponentially in the last few minutes. How could she? How could she talk to Chelsey about such things and not even mention it to her? The pizza came. They ate in almost silence. Chelsey was not going to be waylaid. Could she go to the party, or not?

"Let's see what your father has to say about it, shall we?"

Lavinia was lost in thought, wasn't ready for a discussion about teenage parties at the moment. She had other things on her mind. Her sister-in-law had side-tracked her on the date issue and on the bridesmaid issue.

Who had she talked to about the venue? Probably just about everyone except her. She was so malicious.

No matter. I stand above it, thought Lavinia, *knowing full well she didn't.*

They had a huge ice cream dessert and called a taxi to take them home. Once home, Lavinia settled in for the evening with a whiskey ginger, and Chelsey went up to her room to plan her outfit for the party. She knew she would be able to get around her father.

2/TWELVE
Connor's Conscience

"We'll not be needing the table next week, Toby," Janice said as she stood at the bar. She had arrived early in order to settle the matter with Toby before everyone got there. She wanted to surprise them with her idea.

"Taking a week off, are you?" he asked, although he could guess why she didn't want to be here. Tim had asked him if he could have the use of the restaurant part of the pub for his stag night. Janice was the last person who should be around.

"Yes. I'm treating the group to something special," she said with a twinkle in her eye. With that, she walked off towards the table, just in time to arrive before Andrew and Tina.

They always arrived together now, though no-one could notice any other real change in their relationship. They were obviously close, but not really intimate. Time only for a quick hello before the door opened and in walked Heather, who held the door open for someone behind her. It was Lavinia.

"Where's Connor?" asked Tina. She seemed curiously uneased by the fact that he was not there.

"Maybe he's remembered it's his round first," Andrew meant this as a joke, but somehow it went down like dead duck.

"I'll bring forward mine. He can take the next one. Same as usual, everyone?" Heather was contemplating having something stronger than her lemonade and lime today, so she was actually quite pleased that she could start with it – maybe a red wine. Why not?

She wandered off to the bar and ordered. Toby smiled at her and noted the change in the order. He knew it was her drink that had changed, he just didn't know why. Yet. By the time she got back to the table with the drinks, Connor had made his entrance. He was ruffled somewhat, not only in appearance. Heather felt for him. She really liked the lad. "You had us worried for a minute," she said, "Here's your pint of bitter. Enjoy."

For a moment, they thought he would down it in one, but he stopped just short of it. "How is everyone?" he asked as if nothing was amiss.

"We're all good, and you?" this was Tina. She really cared for Connor. He was a tower of strength as far as she was concerned. Always so open and understanding. So calm and collected.

"I'm fine," unconvincing. The faces of the group showed him that no-one, but no-one believed him.

"Oh bugger, you lot. Leave me alone, I'm fine. Having a bad day, that's all. I'm going to get myself an interim beer. Anyone else?"

They all shook their heads and waited for him to be out of earshot before they began."What's the matter with him? Anyone know?" "Beats me. I only know him from these evenings here. Don't even know where he lives. Now I come to think of it." "He lives on the hospice grounds. He's a resident carer." "Does he have a girlfriend?" "It was his parents he was trying to impress with his cooking skills."

The pub wasn't busy yet, and a beer was quickly pulled. Connor was already back at the table. They all looked at him in expectation. He could see there was no way out of this. Actually, he had known that all along. Truth be known, he had wanted them to push him into telling them. He knew himself, he knew that he would only tell them if they pushed him. That was part of the problem, wasn't it?

"I was at my parents' at the weekend. They had invited a few neighbours over for drinks and thought I should join them."

"Sounds like an excellent move, Connor. Were you not estranged from them for ages?" Tina remembered the little he had told them during the cookery course.

"Yes. I was. And yes, I thought it was a step in the right direction - the direction of normality. It wasn't. The problem was twofold. My parents had spun this story about me, about where I had been, and what I had done and how brilliant I am. It was more than embarrassing. Hardly a word was true. In fact, the only part that was true was that they had had little contact with me for a few years. The reason for the lapse in contact was, however, much more positive from their side of the fence. They even had photos on the side tables and in the hall. Old photos of me, positioned around to make everything look as normal as possible. They were in denial."

"It was probably their way of dealing with the situation," suggested Lavinia.

"It was an illusion. A parallel world they had set up and enjoyed while I was away, and they were trying to align it with the present in such a way as for it to look good, for it to be something that could be presented to the neighbours and the outside world. I couldn't believe it."

"How did you react?" Tina was now worried he had stomped out, and everything was back to square one with his parents.

"I played along for a while. Told a few lies, hid a few facts, showed my compliant side and acted as they wished. For a while. Then, I pretended I felt ill, and left. Actually, I did feel ill, just not in the way I said."

"So, everything is back on hold, is it?"

"With my parents, it is. I haven't spoken to them since. They have tried to call me, but I have been too busy to call back. That's my story, and I'm sticking to it."

"Is it that you don't know how to tell them how you feel, or what?"

"No. Unfortunately, it is not that simple. Here comes the crunch – here's the bit I've been dreading ever since I started at the hospice."

He paused to drink up his beer. "Drink up, my round. I'll tell you when I get back – same as usual for all? Oh, no. You're on red wine today, are you, Heather? No prob." And off he went.

"Poor Connor," said Lavinia. "Must be awful to be in a predicament like that. Fancy having parents like that."

"There must be more to it. He's obviously struggling with something, isn't he? And it doesn't sound like it is only his parents."

"Parents can be bummers, you know," Andrew knew all about that.

"Or just misunderstood," added Tina.

"Or a smoke screen to hide the real problem," Janice could be relied on to find something like this to say.

Lavinia repeated herself, "Poor Connor," as he arrived with the tray of drinks.

"I don't need your sympathy. Have brought this all on myself. Back at home, sitting in the flat, I got to thinking. What my parents were doing, had been doing was not much different to what I have been doing. They created a new reality for themselves, which was easier to deal with. I did, too. They struggled to come to terms with things. I did, too. And you know what? I thought I was doing grand. I thought I was a good example of how to get back on track."

"What do you mean, back on track?"

"Don't interrupt him, Tina. Let him talk."

"Just ask yourselves, how much do you all know about me? We did our cookery course together; we sit here every week together. We talk about everything, settle our worries and lay our thoughts out in the open. And me? What do I do? I listen, I understand, I help maybe even. But I don't open up. You don't know how hard it was for me to accept that this is what I have been doing. But it is exactly what I have been doing. Talk, talk and say only what you want the others to hear."

"What bomb are you going to drop on us, Connor?"

"Leave him, Tina. He has to do this in his own time."

"When I started at the hospice, the Matron was the only one who knew where I had come from. She was the only one who knew about my past. She kept it to herself and she put trust in me. I proved to her that I was worthy of that trust. Because of that, I felt I was doing grand. I managed to recover from everything, even to the extent that I wanted to have contact with my parents again. That was her doing, too. And, of course, Finn. Without Finn, I would not be here now."

"Who`s Finn? You`ve never mentioned him before? Who is he?"

"For Christ`s sake, Tina. Shut up."

"He`s a social worker. My social worker." The group looked at each other.

"I dropped out of school just before the exams. Not because I couldn`t handle them, or couldn`t handle the pressure, I was just fed up with my life as it was. I was fed up with my parents, who, at least that was how I saw it, had no time for me, in fact, no interest in me whatsoever. It seemed like a good idea at the time. Just walk off. Let them fret about where I was and what I was doing. I had my life to lead, and I was going to do it."

Even Tina fell silent. He was on a roll, he needed to let this out.

"I walked the streets in my home town was a stupid idea, didn't take me long to realise that. Stupid because I was still too close, still within reaching distance, still in the vicinity of my home. People knew me. I had to go further afield where no-one knew me, and no-one felt obliged to help me or inform my parents of my handlings.

There was always someone who would offer me a place to stay for the night, or a meal. I had to move on. No way was I going to give in, admit that I had been wrong. That would have proven they were right, wouldn`t it? That was how I saw it. Them or me, one side had to give, and I didn't intend it to be mine. Problem was, the places where no-one knew me were the places where I knew no-one. In fact, places I didn't know. That was a crunch time, believe me there."

If Connor had been sitting next to her, Tina would have touched him in some way, she felt so moved by what he was saying. Janice, who was sitting to his right, did nothing, just stared onto the table, into her glass. Heather, on his left side, turned to look him in the eye and made a face which assured him she wasn't judging him, she was feeling for him.

He continued, knowing it was not only the right thing to do, but it was also essential that he got it out of his system. If he could finally tell them, at least the core story he could be more open with others, as well.

"I'll cut a long story short – keep the details for a later date, maybe - I fell, I fell badly. I thought I had reached rock bottom. Thought life couldn't get much worse. What I didn't know then was that it could have got a whole load worse. Then I met Finn. He listened to me, really listened. He showed me the way back, not back to my parents, he could see that was not a viable option, at least not immediately. The way back into society."

Conor stopped. The next bit was going to be the hardest. He really didn't know how they would react. He took at gulp of beer. This pint was definitely short – the glass was almost empty already. There was no help to be had from the group. They sensed the foreboding and sat, awaiting what would come next. Each sipped at their drink. It looked as if it was going to be a three-round evening.

"He registered me for rehab (pause). I wasn't actually an addict. I hadn't got that far (Connor felt this piece of info was immensely important to the tale), but I had been in contact with drugs, so I had to do this therapy in order to go on to the next step (another pause, another gulp) This is rather difficult to talk about."

Andrew saw the nigh-on empty glasses and decided they could all do with an extra drink tonight. "My round, who's in?"

Everyone nodded.

"Same as usual?"

Heather pointed to her red wine. Tina was ready for a gin and tonic. All the others nodded. Off he went to the bar. When he returned he noticed that all was silent at the table. They hadn't said a word since he left.

"Cheers."

After a swift gulp, Connor was ready to continue. "I'm going to cut another long part-story short. After the rehab, Finn found a job, including a training course for me at the hospice. The Matron was very sceptical at first. Finn assured her that I had never had a drug problem and that the therapy was purely preventive in nature. He told her my story and explained how different I was to other dropouts. He was convinced he had found me in the nick of time, before any harm could have been done. It was his firmness of belief in me that persuaded her to give me a chance. I wasn't going to let him down. I had buggered up my life, and he was my rescuer."

Andrew felt some relief to the tense atmosphere was needed. He held up his glass.

"Well, here's to Finn, then. Thank God he was around."

"Cheers!"

"How come you never mentioned any of this before?" asked Janice, genuinely interested in the answer.

"I was ashamed, I guess. I just didn't want to admit to it. I thought I had proven to myself I could get back, I was proud of myself. I was happy in my job, wanted to preserve the life I had. I wanted to shut the past out, pretend it hadn't been what it was. But you can't do that. You can't build a future on a past that doesn't exist. You only have a future when you face the past – the past as it really was."

Heather felt a strange pang in her stomach.

Connor continued, "The credibility gap you have to deal with is not easy. If you have any kind of conscience, that is. I realised that only too clearly when I was at my parents` do. They were closing their eyes to the reality, pretending it all hadn`t happened. Hadn`t happened the way it had. They had managed to create their own truth to fit their lives. I had, too. But what have I gained if I am like them? What was it all for? What purpose had it served? Do you get me?"

"Oh, I get you," said Heather, spoken from the heart.

"I get you, too, Connor," said Tina. "I am so glad you have told us."

"You sure know how to surprise people," said Janice, regretting it the minute she had "I mean, we never would have guessed any of this." She wasn`t making it much better, so she stopped.

"We don`t think any less of you now. You need to know that. I`m sure I speak for the whole group."

Lavinia had never before felt so moved by a story. She was sincerely impressed by the honesty which flowed through what Connor had told them. She was actually impatient to know more. To know the details he had left out. She had two children of her own, and she had a family life which was, to a certain extent, reliant on what the neighbours thought. She wanted to know.

"You definitely speak for us all there, Lavinia. Here I was thinking I had a problem just because my degree doesn`t hold any scrutiny."

"Cheers!"

The glasses were nearly empty, yet again.

Janice knew they were nearing the time when they would go home, so she had to make her speech now. "Listen up, everyone. I have an announcement to make!"

Surprised looks all round. "I have told Toby we wouldn`t be needing the table next week." The looks got even more surprised.

"I thought we could have a special evening next week. I'm not one for hen parties, so I've thought of something else. I do hope you're all okay with it."

The surprised looks turned into smiles.

"How about you all come to my place, and we cook something together? It would have to be something with minced meat, of course. Just like during the course. What do you think?"

"Brilliant idea, I'm in."

"Me, too."

"Me, too – and Tina, of course."

"What are we going to cook?" asked Connor, as if that were a criterion to be contemplated before joining.

"How about the ratatouille? That was my meal, wasn't it?"

"I thought Tina's stuffed peppers were better, actually."

"Me, too."

"That's it, then. Stuffed green peppers it is. My place, next Wednesday at 6.00 pm. I'll send you all a message with the exact address."

Sadie, back on Smoke Room bar duty, smiled as the group left and cocked her head to the right and lifted her shoulder in the direction of Connor. He smiled back. They stood for a few seconds, just looking at each other. Then Connor left.

Toby was gobsmacked: an ex-druggy working at the hospice. My God, if that wasn't a turn-up for the books! He must have misheard. That didn't seem possible

And Connor, he was such a lovely lad. Would you believe it? Being able to keep things to yourself for so long. Of course, Toby felt he had known all along that there was something strange about Connor. He just couldn't pinpoint it. But drugs, no. He would never have thought that.

Maybe he was wrong? Maybe he just hadn't overheard enough of what Connor was saying. Had missed some crucial parts of the sentence. He had been unusually close to the group all evening, though. Partly because Sadie was here to help out – she seemed particularly interested in this bar today. Funny

That wasn't the real reason he had hung around them, though. He needed their proximity. He needed them. Wasn't easy to actually admit this to himself, but he was jealous of this group. They had what he wanted. They had what he felt he needed and didn't have, couldn't get. They had each other. This "each other" was beyond their families and their loved ones. It was indeed a special type of friendship. A type of friendship which one may crave for, and which many never find. What they gave each other was priceless.

Those who find that within their marriage, or partnership, or circle of friends are blessed indeed, Toby thought. *I need to get a life.*

2/THIRTEEN
Meanwhile, behind the bar

Toby loved his pub. It was damned hard work, with excruciating hours, but he loved it. At first, he had shared his life there with Trish. She was the perfect hostess, the perfect landlady. She was a good-looker, could chat easily to others, would flirt a little with the regulars, was organised, kind, friendly and

And what?

Unfaithful, that's what she was. They had known it would be hard work, and they had decided, together, that they wanted this. It had been his money they put into the project and all had worked out well. The pub was a thriving business. He thought she shared his feeling of achievement, that she was happy with it, enjoying it, and

And what?

Deceitful, that's what she was.

She wanted out, wanted to leave. Claiming she had worked just as hard to get the pub to where it was today, she expected to be paid off with half of the present value of the business. There was no way he could manage that. No way could he find that kind of money to pay her out. He was ruined. It wasn't even his fault. She was the one playing around. She was the one putting everything at risk. That was it – he stood to lose everything, and she would simply pull in a financial gain and push off to enjoy her life further. He would end up with nothing. Nothing but a heap of - nothing.

He felt distraught, out of his depth, and lonely. Very lonely.

She was even holding him back when it came to new relationships. He was scared, scared of being hurt, let down, or even ridiculed. He fancied that Rachel lady who came in every Saturday lunchtime, and he was sure she wasn't completely uninterested. He could sense it in the way she smiled at him. He heard she was a widow, that would explain the two wedding rings on her finger. He had overheard her talking to her friend about some Edmund chap, but it seems he was not really on the cards. He just couldn't bring himself to make a first move. What if he were mistaken? No, it wasn't possible to misinterpret such vibes. She was interested. He would ask her out on a date. He would take an evening off (must be possible with such a good team behind him), and take her out. He felt better already. She would be perfect for him. He would have someone to share his dreams again, share his life. Wouldn´t that be grand?

He decided to make his move on Saturday. He would win her over. Plus, whilst in this positive state of mind, he decided to seek the advice of a lawyer. It could not be that Trish had such a claim on his livelihood. He was certain she just thought he wouldn't oppose her, wouldn't want to foot the expense of a lawyer to counter her attack. She had actually even suggested he shared hers. No way he would fight this battle. And he would win.

2 / FOURTEEN
The "hen party" that wasn`t

Andrew walked out of the staff entrance and turned to walk towards the carpark where he was to be picked up by Tina. They were heading to Janice`s house for the "minced meat revival" evening. There was no way you could get to the house by bus, well no way that would take less than 90 minutes. By car, they could be there in 20 minutes, at max.

As he rounded the corner, he saw Tina in conversation with his boss, William. They knew each other? More than knew, it seemed, as they parted, they kissed each other on the cheek. What the heck was this? Andrew stopped in his tracks. This was a scenario he had not foreseen. What a turn-up for the books this was. Now everything made sense. He hadn`t been offered the new job for his competence, it was Tina pulling in favours. All of a sudden, he didn`t know if he wanted to travel with her, after all. He just stood there. Paralysed.

When Tina saw him, she smiled and waved and then got back into the car, waiting for him to come over. She pressed the ignition, the car started up – but no Andrew arrived. She looked across her shoulder, and he was still standing where he had been before. What the hell was wrong with him? She waited for what seemed like an age. Eventually, he opened the passenger-side door but didn`t get in.

"What was that?" he demanded to know.

"What was what?"

"You and William."

"Me and …. Bill. He`s our neighbour`s son, we grew up together. What`s your problem?"

"Oh, Bill, is it?"

"Calm down, Andrew, what is wrong with you? You're not jealous, are you? There's no need. I haven't seen him for years."

"You can go tell that to your…" he couldn't finish his sentence.

Tina butted in, "We lost contact when he moved out. I really don't see what your problem is."

"Okay, you asked for this – did you talk to him about me?"

"No, I didn't. Why should I? I congratulated him on the new baby, and we talked about his parents. They are friends of my parents."

"Swear it, Tina. Swear you didn't talk to him about me. This is important."

"I swear."

Andrew got in the car. "Okay. Let's go. Can't keep Janice waiting, can we? We can continue this conversation some other time."

The drive was a silent affair, bar the Sat Nav giving instructions. Neither of them had ever been in this part of town. If there had been professional football players in town, this is where they would have found their future homes. Each house, larger and finer than the next, with SUVs galore in front of the garages. Tina pulled up outside No. 16.

"Posh,"

she said, and Andrew agreed. They walked up to the front door and rang the bell.

Janice was uneasy. At the time she had invited them for the "minced meat revival" as she was now calling it, it had seemed a good idea. Now, she wasn't so sure. Was it not part of the flair surrounding their group relationship that they didn't really know each other? None of them had any real contact outside the course – and, of course, now the weekly meetings at the pub. That was what made it all special. Was she forfeiting this tonight?

She opened the door and greeted Tina and Andrew warmly.

"So glad you`re here at last," she said.

"Are we late?"

"No, no. You`re the first to arrive. Come in."

Andrew knew then, Janice had never really changed. She still had that knack of articulating in such a way that people would always misunderstand her.

Coats hardly hung up, the doorbell rang again. It was Lavinia. She opened her arms and embraced Janice as if they were best friends forever.

"Lovely house, Janice, I had no idea." She looked around the hallway in awe and was having difficulty not to show a pinch of envy. Her eyes betrayed her, but no-one was looking too closely, so she got away with it. They walked across into the kitchen – not normally the route one would take when visiting, but they were here to cook together.

Everything was laid out on the mid-room counter, awaiting preparation

The doorbell rang again. The last two guests arrived.

Heather had driven by the Woolpack and picked up Connor. Surprised as she was that he should wish to be picked up there, she hadn`t said anything on the phone. Merely that she would send a WhatsApp to let him know she had arrived outside; she didn`t want to go in. She didn`t have to wait for long. Connor was already standing at the door in conversation with Sadie, the barmaid. She also didn`t have to wait for long for him to explain why he was at the pub. He was on cloud nine. After he had left the pub last week, he had noticed the attention she was giving him and had, plucked all his courage together and returned on Thursday to see if he was picking up the correct vibes. He had been.

Sadie had arranged with Cath that she should do her Wednesday lunchtime shift so she could go out for lunch with Connor. It hadn´t been easy, Connor said. Cath didn't want to swap because Wednesday lunchtime was when Jack was free, and, well, they were "romantically involved," was how she put it. Toby didn't know, and they wanted to keep it that way, at least for a while, till they really knew it was something serious.

When Connor mentioned "Jack," Heather almost ran into the car in front of her. She hadn't noticed that the lights had turned red.

"What did you just say?"

"Cath and Jack are a pair – a clandestine affair – they don't want Toby to know just yet."

"Who is Jack?"

"He works at the pub, too. You must have seen him. He's the handyman. Toby's right-hand man."

"No, I don't know him."

"Lunch was great, she's such good company."

Connor's only interest was Sadie, he had no time for thoughts on Cath, or Jack, or anyone else for that matter.

The rest of the journey found them both drowned in their own thoughts and was, thus, silent, bar the Sat Nav giving instructions.

"Your forecourt is full. I've parked on the kerb, is that okay?" asked Heather.

"Sure, no problem whatsoever. Come on in."

They had to wait for a while till Connor got to the door. He was carrying a rather large box which he had retrieved from the boot of the car.

"What on earth is that?" asked Janice.

"Wait and see!"

Before they started shelling the peppers and preparing the minced meat filling, they toasted the bride-to-be. Janice had poured champagne for all. *Just a sip, we'll watch our alcohol input later.*

They had almost forgotten how much fun it was cooking together. Time sped by, and the alcohol flowed. For half of the visitors, this was not going to be a problem, and for the other half, it was a problem which they had decided would be solved later. They were enjoying themselves.

Within an hour, they were seated at the dining room table enjoying "stuffed peppers with rice" as if it were an emperor's feast. Lavinia noticed, not without a further pang of envy, that the cutlery, crockery and glasses were of the finest quality. In fact, the plates were exactly the ones which she had been admiring in town last week. The (expensive) wine flowed. Even Andrew and Connor were drinking wine tonight, quite a premiere.

Then, Heather stood up and collected the box which Connor had carried into the house earlier. She beamed at Janice and handed it to her. "This is our wedding present for you. We wish you all the very best for your future with Tim. We are all really happy for you."

Janice was quite taken aback. Smiling is not a strong enough word to describe what her mouth was doing. She opened the box to find a meat-grinding machine. What a grand idea!

"So you will never forget how we all first met."

"How could I ever do that?"

As dinner was over, they all moved into the lounge, a large room across the back of the house with an adjacent conservatory.

"Goodness me, Janice. You know how to live!" said Lavinia.

"How could you possibly have contemplated giving all this up?"

"I didn't. You are so materialistic, Lavinia. It is you who is hard to take, you know. It was Tim who left me, remember? Out-of-the-blue, off he went."

She suddenly recalled the hurt, the incomprehension of the whole situation those few weeks ago. She felt tears swelling in her eyes but was determined not to cry. It didn't work. They streamed down her cheeks. "And anyway, he left me the house, didn't he?"

Heather thought she should join in the conversation but missed her cue, and by the time she had something to say, Janice was crying.

"It's okay to be nervous when the big day gets close. You'll find you'll be doing quite a bit of crying over the next days. It is a big thing, you know. By the way, are Tim's parents coming to the wedding? It is next Wednesday, after all. Surely, they must have decided by now."

"So far, it looks as though it is Tim and I with Dylan, plus my Dad and his new lady-friend. But Tim's parents are coming over at the weekend - or drinks on Sunday morning. I guess they'll be telling us then. It'll be thumbs up, or thumbs down. Why they can't just call us on the phone and tell us, I don't know. I'm not looking forward to having them here. I can tell you that."

"Sounds to me like they want to make a mends. Otherwise, they really could just call, couldn't they? Do give them a chance, Janice. Life will be so much easier if you have them on your side."

"Easier said than done," said Janice, which left Heather in a very thoughtful state of mind because she remembered that she, too, had said exactly that to herself just a few weeks ago. And now look – Cath's Jack wasn't her Jack at all. She had jumped the gun. How could she have been so stupid? How could she have thought for a second that her Jack would do such a thing?

One thing this had taught her, though, was that she wouldn't be telling Jack about Eamon. It would do too much damage to the trust that they had built up between them over the years. One silly mistake and all that should go down the drain?

NO, she couldn't risk it. And anyway, as Connor had said, if the man in question was no longer in the vicinity – why rattle any chains? Good old Connor. Where was he?

He was sitting in the armchair in the corner, staring out into the garden. He was actually considering asking about using the hot tub but concluded that it was maybe a tick too forward.

Then Heather walked up behind him.

"All right for some, isn't it? Fancy having a hot tub in the garden."

"Who needs one? You can have a grand life without one. I'm sure of that."

"Certainly, if you have the right partner to share your life with. I'm very happy for you, Connor."

Tina was in earshot and looked up at this last sentence: "You have a partner?"

"Not exactly. Not yet. But Sadie - you know her from the Woolpack – and I are dating. She is just the type I have been looking for all this time. Don't know how come I didn't see it before."

Tina wondered if it was the alcohol which made her feel so queasy all of a sudden. Connor had a girlfriend! Why was she so surprised? Why was she so …. moved, sad even? She walked away so that Connor would not see in her face how she had been affected by this piece of news.

Seeing her walk towards the French windows Andrew followed her. He was genuinely sorry for the way he had spoken to her before. He had been too quick off the mark, much too fast to believe the worst. Truth be known it was his lack of confidence in himself which had led him to believe that Tina had anything to do with his promotion. He could hardly believe it had been off his own bat. He needed to talk to her – today – to make sure she realised this.

He had had too much to drink, that was for sure, but he was convinced that he could string enough words together to ensure Tina understood he was sorry.

"Work was exhausting today. I'm afraid you got the raw end of the stick earlier. Sorry."

"It's okay. I should have realised sooner that Bill was actually the boss you were talking about, but you kept saying William and I never twigged. Not important, though, is it?"

"No, not at all. Much more important that the company gets their act together."

"What do you mean?"

"I told you I had suggested a job share. They're about to bugger it up."

"You mean your contract is no longer valid?"

"No, my contract is fine. It's Sam's they are fooling with."

"I thought everything was settled. I was really proud of you, you know. Standing up for your co-workers like that. Even forgoing part of the glory."

"Guess you never know what will happen when women get involved."

"Sorry?"

"Yeah. Sam said I had got a full contract and training out of the deal, and all she had got was training. She wanted more money for the responsibility of being acting Assistant Manager. She even went so far as to say the only reason they weren't giving her extra money was because she was a woman. The whole thing has completely backfired."

Lavinia was there like a shot.

"Probably right in that. Always is the way, you know."

Tina walked over to the drinks tray. She needed a drink. Sam was a woman. She didn't think she could take too many more surprises today. That funny feeling of fifteen minutes ago returned. She was again moved and sad.

Janice was the one who had probably drunk the least all evening, but she had a distinct feeling it was time to finish the party. Everyone had drunk far too much, not that she minded, but she could feel that things were about to get out of control, at least emotion-wise. Lavinia was on a roll, Connor was mooching, Tina was sulking, Andrew was wishing he'd kept his mouth shut after all, and Heather was miles away.

It had been a gamble bringing them here tonight. It had worked out, but she felt she shouldn't push her luck too far.

She suggested she call taxis for everyone

Lavinia refused – she would call Ian, he could come and pick her up. He could come and see where she had spent the evening.

Heather refused – she would call Jack, he could come and pick her up. She felt the need to be with him.

Tina accepted, as did Andrew and Connor. One taxi would be enough, he could drop them off one after the other.

Janice was slightly disturbed by the mood of the group as they left. Was it the unusual amount of alcohol in play, or was it the unprecedented proximity that had changed things? She hoped it was the alcohol, but she wasn't at all convinced.

2/FIFTEEN

Meanwhile, the five meet

Toby was surprised to see Heather coming to the pub on a Friday evening. All the more surprised to see her followed in by Andrew and Tina. As Lavinia joined them a few minutes later, he was beginning to think he was going senile, and it wasn`t Friday, after all. Maybe he should go and tell Connor they were here. Connor was out at the rear door of the pub talking to Sadie. He needn`t have considered it. Connor turned up of his own accord. They were lucky the table was free, up until literally ten minutes before the group from the lawyer's office on Waymore Street had been sitting there. Once they were all seated, Andrew stood up and checked orders for drinks, walked over to the bar and placed the order with Toby.

"I`ll bring them over to you," said Toby.

"Okay. Fine, thanks," a rather taken-aback Andrew replied as he wandered back to the table. "Toby says he`ll bring the drinks over so we can get straight down to business," he smiled at the group to ensure that everyone knew he was actually in a good mood.

"Everyone got over their hangovers?" Connor asked.

"Took me a while, I can tell you. Wine is not my thing. I walked around like a zombie for most of yesterday."

"You need to get more practice in," Lavinia said with a laugh, "or give up completely."

"Or, discipline yourself," added Heather.

"Beers for the men, g & t for Lavinia, lemonade and lime for Heather, and lager and lime for you, Tina."

Toby placed each drink in front of its rightful owner. "So, what brings you lot here on a Friday evening? Not that I`m complaining, like."

"We`re planning to surprise Janice and Tim next Wednesday," Tina explained. "They're getting married sometime in the afternoon – we still have to find out exactly when – and we want to be there when they come out of the registry office."

"What a grand idea," said Toby. "If you let me join you, I reckon I could be persuaded to part with the piece of information you are lacking."

With that, he sat down on the vacant chair. No-one was about to contradict. "3.00 pm it is. I heard Tim say so on Wednesday – he was here for his stag night. My God, what an evening that was."

"No gaudy details, please," said Lavinia as she glanced over to the door which had just opened. In walked Rachel, their cookery course teacher. The group looked at each other in amazement.

"Oh, hi," said Toby, walking over to her. He placed a rather shy kiss on her left cheek. "I wasn`t expecting you till 7ish."

"Am I interrupting something?" she asked, adding, "Oh, my God, it is you lot. What a coincidence. How lovely it is to see you all here. How wonderful that you are still meeting up."

Toby was now even more surprised. "You know each other, then?"

"Rachel was our cookery course teacher," explained Heather. "She`s the one who brought us all together."

"My goodness me, the world really is small, isn`t it?"

"Especially around here it is," added Andrew.

Toby was hesitant, wasn`t sure if he should sit back down again, or not.

"Well, she could come with us to the registry office then, couldn`t she?"

Connor stood up and grabbed a chair from the next table. "Sounds like an excellent idea."

Rachel looked puzzled, but sat down on the chair that was being pushed under her.

Toby sat down again, and Lavinia took over the conversation.

"Okay, so now we know that they have their appointment at 3."

Seeing the look on Rachel's face, she quickly added,

"Janice! Janice and Tim are getting married next Wednesday."

Rachel beamed.

"I've had an idea what we could do, or does anyone else want to start?"

No-one offered the slightest impression of wanting to undertake any interruption. If Lavinia had an idea, that was fine with them.

"Ribbon wands,"

she said and waited for a reaction. There was none.

"Ribbon wands."

she repeated.

"No idea what that is," admitted Andrew

"Me neither,"

said Connor. "Join the club," said Heather. Tina just nodded.

Toby smiled at Rachel, who smiled back.

"I have a photo here for you. This is what they look like."

She passed her mobile phone around the table.

"Sticks with ribbons on the end? What on earth would we do with those?" asked Andrew.

We greet Janice and Tim by waving with them when they come out of the building. Confetti isn`t allowed, but these make no mess whatsoever."

"I`m not going prance around waving a silly stick with ribbons on the end. You can count me out there," Connor obviously was against the idea.

"It could be a laugh," said Toby. " Don`t be a spoiled sport."

"It`s different, I`ll give you that," Tina was, at least, willing to consider the idea.

"In the face of a lack of other suggestions, we have to think this through," Heather was in organising modus. "So, we all have these ribbon wands and wave them around when the happy couple leave the building, right? Just like we used to do with confetti, is that the idea?"

"Yes," Lavinia was pleased someone was taking this seriously. "I can go over to the wholesale market tomorrow and get some, that`s not a problem. I have checked, and they have some in stock. I reserved ten, but I guess fourteen will be okay, too."

"Don`t bother for me. I don`t need any. I`ll come along, I`ll shout "hurrah" as loud as the next one, but I`m not waving wands around like a mad Morris dancer," Connor stopped himself, verbally expanding on this thought.

"I`m with Connor on this, so your ten will be fine. Toby seems okay with it, he can prance around as much as he likes."

"What colour are the ribbons?" Rachel wanted to know.

"I ordered in white. Thought that was best. Don`t know if Janice has a colour scheme, and white would fit with any colour, wouldn`t it?"

"May I make a suggestion? I don`t want to butt in, but maybe this idea would help." Toby's breast swelled, he really did like this woman a lot.

"Looks like we might need some assistance here, indeed," said Heather

"Well, how about we all have these ribbons wands and stand five a side to the door as they come out. Andrew and Connor stand on each side of the door and hold a white band across the entrance so that they have to cut it to get through. Like a sort of symbolic entrance into married life?"

Toby looked at Rachel. The ladies looked at Andrew and Connor and were relieved when Connor said, "Okay. I`ll bring the scissors."

Tina knew someone who worked in the same building as the registry office. She would see if she could get them to instruct one of the guests to ensure that Tim and Janice left the building in front of the others.

"My round," said Lavinia and Toby got up to get the drinks. He knew what everyone wanted. When he returned to the table with the drinks, he caught Rachel saying, "Yes, I know him well. I`m sure he`ll come. It is a novel idea, and Tim and Janice are both quite well-known in the town, so it would be of a certain common interest. I`m sure I can get him to come and take photos for the newspaper.

They all drank to their successful plan.

"Does anyone know if Tim`s parents are coming to the wedding?" asked Heather. No-one, not even Toby, knew this. This was something which they would find out on Wednesday.

After finalising the arrangements for Wednesday, Toby returned to the bar, and Rachel followed him there a short while later.

The Six- reduced-to-five-pack left the pub, agreeing to meet in front of the registry office at 3.00 pm. Not earlier, just to make sure that Janice was unaware of their intention.

2/SIXTEEN

Janice's Joy

The sun shone brightly, not a cloud in the sky. Janice and Tim walked up to the registry office with Dylan between them. Inside the building, they met up with John, Janice's Dad and his new lady-friend, Sandra. Expectancy hung in the air, as Tim's parents were not there yet. Then the door opened and in they walked. They approached the group hand-in-hand as if giving each other the strength to see this through. Janice and Tim had smiles for everyone, in abundance. Nothing was going to spoil this. Punctually, at three o'clock, the door to the actual registry office opened, and they all walked in. The ceremony was simple, just as they wanted it. They were married. They walked out of the room, hand-in-hand. With this, they were giving each other the strength to face the world together They were so happy Dylan had even planted a smile on his face, and slowly but surely, he felt it had a right to be there. There were kisses and good wishes all round. Next stop was the "Shipwell Manor House Hotel," for champagne and a dinner to remember. Janice's Dad let them pass and stood in the way of Tim's parents getting to the door first.

They walked over to the exit, opened the door and were faced with a wide white ribbon blocking their exit. Puzzled, they looked at each other.

"To enter into your life together, you must cut through this ribbon, and may all good fortune be with you," they heard in a voice that Janice recognised as Connor's. His face appeared, beaming, on the right of the door. Then Andrew's appeared to the left of the door. They took the scissors from Connor and cut through the ribbon, only now seeing that all the others were standing as in a guard of honour and then starting waving and shouting at them. Even Rachel was there, my God, and Toby as well! She embraced all of them in turn, this was overwhelming. Tears ran down Janice's face. Fortunately, the photographer from the newspaper had already taken his shots. This was to be shared with the town in the Friday issue of the *Town Chronicle*.

Tim was similarly moved by this performance of affection for his "wife." He held her close and kissed her. She was so happy.

She knew she had done the right thing. She had married Tim. She knew she had a wonderful life ahead, with Tim and Dylan. She knew she had the support of people who cared.

She knew the Six Pack was alive and kicking!

PART 3:
The Full Pack - The Milk of Human Kindness

"The Full Pack"

also referred to as "the full package."

Definition:

1) all the elements constituting a whole or occurring as a unit

2) something, or someone that possesses a full set of relevant characteristics, usually desirable ones

3/ONE
Toby's Woolpack

As Toby sat on the ruffled bed, he contemplated his life. His glasses lay on the bedside cabinet, and his face was cupped in his hands. His T-shirt was tucked in his jeans and showed off his slight paunch. He wasn't fat by any stretch of the imagination, but sat as he was, he looked like it. He didn't care; these were his private quarters, he could look how he liked. Living above the pub, he didn't have much private space, only this bedroom, the "snug," the bathroom and the kitchenette. His lounge was the public lounge downstairs. He tilted his head to one side, and grooves appeared on his forehead. He was deep in thought. He knew he should be more than content. He had achieved what he wanted in life – a pub to his name.

Indeed, The Woolpack, was no ordinary pub. It stood in all its glory in the centre of town and was a drinking hole par excellence for numerous members of the town's diverse society. He had bought it for an extremely reasonable – if not to say - cheap – price after leaving the army and had gradually reinstated it as a (if not THE most) popular meeting point in town, for young and old. It had been hard work initially. They (he and his wife Trish) had put in all hours that God had sent to first refurbish the place, and then to ensure that welcoming atmosphere that all pub-goers come to expect from their local. He had a superb team working with him – Jack, his Man Friday; Danny, the chef; Sadie and Cath, the two full-time barmaids; four youngsters from the college who helped out part-time; and now Rachel, as well.

Rachel, now that was a story and a half. She had been a regular visitor for Saturday lunch before he had plucked up enough courage to ask her if she would care to go out for dinner with him. She was a history teacher at the local comprehensive school and she was a widow. They had hit it off from the start and had been "seeing" each other for the past five months now. She had helped Toby overcome his disappointment, turned anger, turned cynicism, of Trish leaving him to spend her life in the sunnier realms of Spain. And now, she was helping him rediscover what love is. The sex was intense in a smooth, warm way – not the wild, rough and tumble as had been with Trish. They weren`t planning to move in together. Neither of them thought that was yet on the cards, but they were planning month by month, what they would do together – how they would enjoy each other`s company to the full. They were creating a foundation of trust on which to build their future.

He had fallen for her. There was no question about that. There was (almost) nothing he wouldn`t do for her. She obviously felt the same, for she had now even offered to work with him on Saturday evenings and Sunday lunch-times to share in his pleasure at seeing the pub thrive.

But - he had a secret. Actually, it wasn`t really a secret, it was a problem. One which he simply hadn`t told her about yet. It wasn`t that he didn`t trust her. It was just that he had to get it sorted first. He didn`t want to trouble her with it. For it had to do with his wife, Trish.

She wanted money. Lots of money. Money he didn`t have. Toby had put all his life savings, plus his retirement money, into the pub business. It was unquestionably a successful business, and he was absorbed in the fulfilment it gave him. For him, it was life as he wanted it. For him, it was the life he had laid out for himself. For him, it was his achievement.

Not so for Trish. As she saw it, it had been a combined effort, and a mighty one at that. She saw herself entitled to half of the pub. Her lawyer encouraged her belief that she could expect to be paid off to the tidy sum of 50% of the market value of the business, and 50% of the revenue to -date, plus an add-on to cover potential income over the coming years, which she would be forfeiting.

Toby couldn`t believe this could be right, but he couldn`t really afford a lawyer himself. He had decided to bluff his way through. He would make an alternative offer and claim to be willing to refrain from taking a lawyer if she accepted, and accepted quickly.

He just couldn`t feasibly assess how low he could go with his offer. He just wasn`t sure just yet how badly she needed the money and how desperate she was to be rid of him, and their mutual past.

Equally difficult was deciding how he would finance any deal. It was, in fact, this part of the problem over which he was losing sleep. At his age, even with a sizable income from the business, he was under no illusion that he could easily get any more money from his bank. And indeed, why should he need to? Hell, this was HIS!

Just as he was about to get up and make his morning cup of tea, the telephone rang. It was Rachel. His spirits rose immediately.

3/TWO
Connor's promise

"Okay, listen to this. I have made one bugger of a promise."

The group looked at Connor with as much curiosity as astonishment.

"Wait till I get back with the drinks. I don't want to miss out on this." Andrew hurried off to the bar to order the usual round of drinks.

Toby knew exactly what it would be: two bitters, one white wine, one gin-and-tonic, one lager-and-lime and one lemonade-and-lime. This was their order: two rounds of it every Wednesday evening. There had been a couple of exceptions. He remembered once when Janice celebrated her engagement and another time when Tina was being bullied at work, but by-and-large, this was their standing order. When they had first started meeting here, Toby had taken ages to figure out how they fit together. They were an unusual group, called themselves the Six Pack as there were six of them. It seems they had done a cookery course together and had decided to meet up ever since. What really threw Toby was when he found out that his Rachel had actually been their teacher in the course. My God, what a small world it was in this mid-sized town nestled in the middle of England.

He watched as Andrew placed the drinks down on the table in the bay window of the "Smoke Room" and mused at the thought that they had no idea just how their conversations carried and just how much of what they discussed he could hear from his position behind the bar. He merely had to stand exactly between the last gin dispenser and the first of the whisky dispensers, and their opinions were his. Unfortunately, tonight, he wouldn't be able to hear much. Sadie and Cath were both busy in the restaurant bar on the far side of the pub. He was alone here. He'd have to be swift to keep up with the orders.

"So," said Andrew. "What have you promised – and who is the lucky person?" "She's not lucky, I can tell you that," answered Connor. "She's a resident at the hospice. She has only weeks to live. I have been sitting with her quite a lot recently. She is such a lovely lady, but it seems she is as good as alone in the world. No -one ever comes to see her. It`s heartbreaking to see. Anyway, she was worried, said she couldn`t go without finding a replacement."

"Replacement for what?" asked Lavinia, eager to know more, but also wary of jumping to conclusions. This had always been her way before the group made her see the error in her ways and had convinced her that she should ask more questions, and assume less.

"Not a what exactly," Connor was fighting some inner strife. "More a who. She`s a Year 3 teacher at the primary school on the Woodford estate. She says most of the kids in her class arrive for school in the morning having had no breakfast."

Janice, who worked in the education department at the local council offices, butted in. "I've heard that too. I just didn't want to believe it."

"This lady certainly has me believing it. She gets really emotional about it. Starts crying and throwing insults at the council for not helping the families."

Heather, who was now in the administration of the local hospital, felt for the children. "How can parents do that? I mean, is it a time problem, or what?"

"From what this teacher tells me, it is in part a time thing, and in part a financial matter."

Tina, a bank clerk, couldn`t believe this. "What! Surely, a bowl of porridge wouldn`t break any bank, would it? Come on, this is ridiculous."

Andrew thought it was time he had his say in the matter, although he wouldn`t dream of saying anything against Tina. "I have noticed recently at the DIY store that money is getting tighter. People are becoming more careful about what they buy. You know really stupidly, like buying tools because they are cheaper, rather than looking at quality. They then end up with gadgets which will break after minimal use."

Lavinia was losing patience somewhat. "Heavens, Andrew, that is in no way comparable. If parents can`t afford to give their kids a breakfast before they go to school, they must be really hard up. They won`t be off down to your DIY store to buy tools, will they?"

"I still don´t see what this has to do with you, Connor, do please explain"

Connor took a deep breath. "Well, my resident, let`s call her Lucy to make things easier, has been helping her class out. She had been bringing in cereals, milk, fruit, and joghurts to school with her. Right up until she collapsed and was taken to hospital, where they made that fateful diagnosis. Now she`s worried the kids aren`t getting any breakfast again."

Janice wanted clarification. "You mean, Lucy bought the food herself and took it into school for them?"

"Exactly."

Tina suddenly realised where this was going. "Connor, what bugger of a promise have you made? What have you promised this Lucy woman?"

"I couldn`t help myself. I felt so sorry for her. This is just so unprofessional, but I said it, I promised. Lucy was getting so worked up, so irate. Yes, I did. I promised to take over."

"How the hell are you going to do that?" Lavinia asked.

"God alone knows," he answered.

"I think we need another round of drinks. Same again, everyone?"

Everyone nodded, and Lavinia walked over to the bar.

"This is crazy. It is crazy to even consider it. There is no way you can nip by the school in the morning and bring 30+ kids some breakfast before you start your shift at the hospice. The logistics, of it alone don`t work, not to mention the finances," this was Tina, ever the banker.

"You can't just turn up at a school and march in anyway," said Janice. She knew all about permits and regulations in dealing with children.

Lavinia returned with the drinks "Okay. Let's look at this realistically, shall we? I have two kids and I know how difficult it is to get them out of bed in time to eat something before they go to school. If I wanted an easy life, I could just leave them there and send them off at the last minute without breakfast, couldn't I? Especially if I knew someone else would give them breakfast later."

Heather agreed on this point. "Emily never gets up on the first call. It takes at least three tries before she gets into the bathroom, and then I have to keep reminding her of the time. She manages a bowl of cereal. I make sure of that. No time for much more, though

Janice agreed to a certain extent. "Getting Dylan up in the morning is sheer hell. It is a fight-and-a-half, but we fight it out every morning. You certainly have to have a determined strength when it comes to ensuring kids leave home in time for school. However, …"

She couldn't finish her sentence because Tina was eager to pitch in. Although she had no children, she did have an opinion about this. "Like you all say, it is a struggle, but you're all doing it, aren't you? That's what parents do. I am wary of putting this all down to a lapse attitude of the parents. I mean, if they just couldn't be bothered to have a row every morning, they could give the kids some sandwiches to take with them, couldn't they? There must be more to it."

Andrew had recovered from his earlier reproach and was ready to try again. "Exactly. Tina's right. There must be more to it. I mean, if the parents can't be bothered to get up themselves, that is a situation you can't change, Connor. If they are too weak to bother with arguing with their kids, that is another area over which you have no influence. However, if it is a money problem, or rather a household budget problem, then we could start to look at it."

"I don't get what you say about the difference between a money problem and a household budget problem," Heather was curious.

"I mean that if it is a money problem, simply more money would help. If it is a household budget problem, it won`t."

"You`re going to have to explain a little more, I`m afraid."

"Okay. Look at it like this. If a family gets a handout, they can decide how to spend it. I`m just suggesting that maybe it will go into the pot set aside for the kid`s breakfasts, but just as maybe, it won`t. Then again, if it is an attitude problem, either of the kids, or their parents, we don`t stand a chance of influencing anything."

"This is all very interesting stuff, but it doesn`t help me with my promise to Lucy, does it?"

"Actually, I think it does," said Janice. "In order to know what to do – how to help - you need to know what the problem actually is. Like I said, I have heard rumours of this scenario at the office, I just didn`t want to believe them. We need to find out, if your Lucy really was helping these kids or was simply encouraging the parents in their failure to do their duty."

"I could talk some more with Lucy and see what she has to say. After all, she knows the kids, and the families."

"And I`ll see what I can find out in the education department. They must have some statistics about all of this."

Lavinia couldn't stop herself from saying, "Bottom line is though, Connor, you have put yourself in a very tricky situation. I mean, your Lucy will never know if you keep your promise, or not. But you will, won`t you? How on earth could you get yourself in this situation? It is completely against all you learnt, isn`t it?"

Heather had a soft spot for Connor. She already knew the real reasons for the lack of breakfasting, indeed the lack of food, on the estate but couldn`t say anything. Her knowledge was based on her experiences whilst working at the doctor`s surgery, she and Dr Brewer (her former lover) had often discussed the situation of many of the families on the Woodford estate. So, she just said, "I`ll see what I can uncover, as well. Let`s postpone any further talk of this until we have more info."

"I reckon that`s a good idea. We don`t want to go rushing into anything here, do we? Conor is going to have to hold himself back a little until we get more info. Just don`t go around making any more promises, mate!" Andrew smiled as he said this, but Connor wasn`t really sure that he meant it humorously.

"I appreciate you all taking this seriously. I really do. I`m in quite a mess about it. I know I should never have promised the likes. I think I can keep myself from making any further commitments – at least until next week," he laughed.

Now it was Andrew`s turn to be puzzled. He didn`t know quite how funny this remark was supposed to be.

There was an awkward silence around the table.

"Just so you all know, by the time we next meet ….." Tina started and glanced quickly at Andrew, who picked up the cue, "I will have moved in with Tina."

They both laughed when they saw the confused reactions of the group members. How come no-one had noticed they had got that far in their relationship? Andrew was ready with an explanation (although not quickly, they both rather enjoyed the fact that everyone had "misunderstood the message). "The bloke I was flat-sitting for has been back for a while, and he was eager to see the back of me. And Tina`s new house has three bedrooms – it`s a house-share, pure and simple."

"Good news, all the same. Congratulations. Seems everything is working out quite well, doesn`t it?"

Tina had bought the house on the outskirts of town only recently. It had been quite an inner struggle for her to finally sign the papers and move away from her parents. But she was really happy with her purchase – it was only an end-of-terrace with a very small garden, but the kitchen was a good size with a dining area extension, and the living room was plenty big enough for her. Upstairs had three bedrooms and a bathroom. Andrew was having two of these rooms; one as his bedroom the other as a living room-cum-study. They had yet to put everything to the test, but they were both convinced this could work out. Their friendship was stable, open and honest. They both felt blessed to have found the other one. With the added advantage of having Andrew pay for the lodgings, thus easing the mortgage load, Tina was sure, nothing could go wrong.

They all drank to the news and left the pub - each of them going their different ways, leading their completely different lives which never crossed, bar their Wednesday evening meetings at the "Woolpack." Except, of course, now Tina and Andrew, who would be living together.

3/THREE
When you`re too busy mopping up

Toby put the cash in the safe and went across the hallway to his bedroom. The bed was still unmade – of course, it was. Who was there to make it up? The day hadn`t gone badly, in fact, the earnings had been good for a Wednesday. All the regulars had been, plus a new group in from the new insurance broker`s office in Paddock Lane. My, could they drink, and that at lunchtime! How on earth they managed to get any work done afterwards was beyond belief.

He hadn`t seen Rachel today, but that was normal for a Wednesday. He had thought about her a lot, though, which was also normal. She was a little older than him, but you`d never know by looking at her. Probably, when seen with her children, she would maybe seem so, that often happens. Not that he minded. He had yet to meet the children, they were both away studying. One of them was even studying for a PhD, so Toby was anxious not to let her down when they did meet up. It made him realise how much he actually missed not having children of his own. Trish had always said it was probably for the better that she couldn`t have kids, and it seems that was quite true, looking at the present situation. Although they would be old enough to fend for themselves by now, it would certainly be a further strain on things if there were children involved. Separations always have a nasty bite. No -one ever really comes out smelling of roses, and there is always plenty of dirty laundry to drag into the open. Just imagine if she were to start calculating time she had spent bringing up children and putting that into the immense equation that she had conjured up with her oh-so-clever lawyer - doesn`t bear thinking about.

He took a sip of the whisky he had brought up with him from the bar. He had taken to this routine recently, although he knew he shouldn`t. He knew it could become the start of a rather unbalanced "friendship," but it did seem to help him fall asleep quicker. That was the end of the positive side, though.

Toby had remembered what his Grandmother had often quoted, "You're too busy mopping up and have forgotten to turn the tap off."

That was how he felt now, so, he had made one decision, at least. He had decided that tonight, he was going to look at the situation from an objective point of view, void of any emotion. He had come to recognise that once he allowed his growing loathe for his wife to enter into the equation, he stopped thinking strategically. He acknowledged that the best idea would be to have someone more objective to help but he couldn't bring himself to confide in anyone, not even Rachel. He knew she would help him figure this mess out, but he couldn't generate the necessary courage to lay this all at her feet. He considered this would be an imposition which their fresh intimacy would surely not survive. Whatever the case, he had decided, he wasn't going to risk it.

His old army comrades would be of no use. Every time he had met them since he left, there was never more than plentiful small talk and plenty of booze. They wouldn't have a clue where to start. Socially, he was isolated. Apart from his pub regulars, who did he have?

As for his family, he knew he could expect no help whatsoever, neither financially nor emotionally. His parents were both dead, his brother was recovering from a massive stroke in a nursing home in Scotland and his sister lived in America with her husband and two children. None of whom he had seen for the last 15 years. Whilst pondering this, he had to admit to himself that, from whatever angle one observed this, he really, he was not a family man. He thought, my God, I am even kidding myself that my brother is "recovering" just to make me feel better. He wasn't recovering at all, he would never recover. He would spend the rest of his days in that nursing home, sitting in his wheelchair and waiting for someone to come and visit him. Toby knew he should go. Sometime. Maybe when all this was settled.

In the meantime, he had to create a strategy. Tonight.

What exactly did Trish want? Last time they had met she had seemed very amiable. She had obviously been instructed to keep things business-like, have no argument, no raised voices, stay calm. She had. She had herself under control. So, she had her strategy all lined-up. She knew what she wanted.

I don't, thought Toby. *I neither know what I want nor do I know what she really wants.*

He found it crushing to accept that she simply wanted out – with the best possible financial settlement. However, he was adamant in his inner acceptance that he, too, wanted out – with the least possible financial strife. There it hit him – a forceful crunch to the brain – step one was already clear.

They both wanted out. They both conceded that their marriage was over. Irrevocably over. No way back.

The hurt

now STOP! A screech came from inside his head. *Tonight is the night where we stick to the facts, remember?*

Fact one: they had been married for 21 years.

Fact two: they had no children.

Fact three: she had been employed at Rothman's for fifteen years.

Fact four: she had left work to come and start up the pub with him.

Fact five: It was his retirement money, and his saving account money that was put into the renovation of the pub.

Fact six: the mortgage on the pub building was in both names.

Fact seven: they had both worked hard …

Fact eight: she had been unfaithful, numerous times.

Fact nine: She had cheated on him.

Fact ten: she had taken money from the business account for personal gain.

Fact eleven: she had made him look like a fool.

Toby found it difficult to get back on track. This was always the case. Every time he thought about Trish, he ended up with him hating her even more. Hating what she had made him endure.

A sip of whisky and fact twelve materialised: their marriage was over, for good. Toby was about to tick off fact thirteen: there was to be a divorce when it suddenly dawned on him that she hadn't actually said that yet. Why had she only said, **it's over**, but never said,

I want a divorce?

Had lightning struck straight into his bedroom at that very moment, he could not have been more shocked.

She doesn't want a divorce. She's going to milk me for all I have, now and in the future. She'll keep coming back for more

Toby downed the whisky and sat on the side of the bed, staring at the wall.

3/FOUR
Zeal without knowledge

Tina placed the drinks tray on the table, and they all took their respective drink from it. Lavinia asked,

"All go well with the move, then?"

"Oh yes, we're all settled already. I didn't have much, no furniture or anything like that. Only my clothes and my computer stuff."

No-one else said anything. Normally, this wouldn't have been the case, but everyone was much too eager to re-engage with the other topic from last week. It was Connor that kicked off with a dampener "I have to tell you that we won't be getting much help from my Lucy. She is really in a bad state; I spoke to her last Friday for a short while, and got a little bit more info, but not too much to go on, really. But, it is all we have to go on – the chances of her becoming more stable are minimal. My goose is well and truly cooked."

"Before we go any further, Connor, we need to know how you stand regarding your promise to your Lucy. Do you really feel bound to it?" Lavinia needed to know this, so she assumed everyone else was asking themselves the same question.

The others weren't actually asking themselves this. The looks on their faces showed this quite clearly.

Ignoring this, Lavinia continued, "Come on. This is important. You made this promise – the woman will be dead within weeks, maybe days. She'll never know whether you kept your promise or not, will she? So, I'm just asking – how serious is this for you?"

"Are you on board or not?" asked Janice, who seemed strangely agitated by the sheer situation of the question being posed at all."

Lavinia was taken aback by this straightforwardness. "I am as on board as everyone else as soon as Connor commits."

"I feel I have to do something. I don`t know what, and I certainly don`t know how, but I have to act in some way. She is relying on me. It is a matter of integrity, of honesty, of decency. I can`t go back on my word."

"Right, that`s it then. Decided – I`m in."

A sigh of relief could be perceived in all except Andrew. He was still to be convinced they could do anything at all. "It is all well and good, giving such a promise, but as you rightly said, you have no idea what you can do, and no idea how to even get started. The way I see it is this: she was worried and shared her torment with you as you sat by her bed. She may very well have known you could not step into her footsteps. Think straight here. She was a teacher – you are not. She worked at the school – you don`t. She knew the kids – you don`t. She had extra cash – you don`t. Do I need to go on?"

Tina jumped in, always willing to help Andrew – her new house-mate. "What Andrew is saying is all correct. It may sound even heartless, but it is correct. We have to stay focussed and keep our heads securely screwed on, not allowing emotions to get in the way. We need to get the facts, assess them, and take it from there. First fact is, Connor has made a promise he wishes to keep."

"I have some more facts for you," Janice had been busy gathering info from the education authority. "There are loads of kids who regularly go to school without breakfast. Some because they can`t be bothered to get up early enough, and some, because there is no breakfast to be had at home. Here, too, there are some parents who can`t be bothered to fix breakfast, some who have already left the house before the kids get up, and others who simply don`t have the money. The department did a survey recently and found out that, on average, 65% of the primary school children on the Woodford estate arrived at school without breakfast. In Year 3, the figure was 70%. This is particularly important because, as of Year 3, they no longer automatically qualify to get free dinners. Only families receiving certain benefits qualify for free dinners after Year two. We are looking at a real problem here."

"I can back that up," said Heather, who had also been busy collecting snippets of info from as many people as possible. "I spoke to my daughter, Emily, about this, she's seven now, and she said in her class, almost everyone had breakfast before they came to school. But at the hospital, when I spoke to some colleagues, they had loads of different tales to tell about the school on the estate. Not many of them positive, I should add. I am wary to say it is a problem at the school, but I do think that there is more to it than just that the children come from households struggling with the bills. Many of the parents work at the factory, and the early shift starts before seven. The children aren't up when they leave the house for work."

Janice was not finished. "Absolutely. From what I hear, though this is not really official, it is more hearsay than anything else, but it does fit: the school is struggling to cope with some of the difficulties they are faced with. Almost all of the teachers hold some kind of extra activity after school hours to ensure that the kids are occupied and are kept off the streets. They are being pushed to their limit already."

"That's as may be, but we can't leave them out of the equation, can we?"

Lavinia said this in such a manner that it was perceived as generally constructive. "As Andrew rightly said, we aren't involved in the school in any way. If we are not careful, we will be seen as the oh-so-high-and-mighty-do-gooders who want to step in and save the world."

"So, we have to get the school involved, then, don't we? Can you do that, Janice?" Tina felt slightly naïve asking this, but someone had to get the ball rolling.

"I think not. If I go, it will be seen as an official act by the education authority, even if it isn't. I can't risk that. Anyway, this is Connor's baby, isn't it? We wouldn't even be talking about this if it weren't for him making promises to a dying old lady."

This proved, once again, to the group that Janice still had the knack of making simple statements sound so terribly negative. They all knew she didn`t mean it the way it had left her mouth. Fortunately, they also knew how to deal with it. They ignored the last part of the speech completely.

"Do you all honestly think I am the right person to go to the school and talk to them about this? They won`t take me seriously, will they? I mean, look at me – I`m much too young for a start. I don`t have kids. I don`t live in the area. I`m a busy-body per excellence for them, aren`t I?"

"I could go with you," Heather had offered before really thinking about the consequences, but it was out now. "If we go together, we tick a few boxes, at least."

"What will you say, though? We don`t have a plan, no strategy. Truth be known, no idea whatsoever as to what we want to do, or how we want to help. Only Connor`s promise and pinch of goodwill. Not enough to approach them yet, if you ask me, I will never forget what one of my lecturers at uni once said – zeal without knowledge is the sister of folly. We should take that to heart, don`t you think?" Andrew was back in the running.

Heather felt more positive, even on the little they had going for them. "Let`s recap: we have Connor`s promise to a teacher at the school. We have the info that kids are coming to school without breakfast. We, as parents, and as concerned members of society, feel we would like to help. Sounds like a good start for an initial meeting to me. And it certainly sounds like the right place to get any further info. We can`t go any further until we know whether the school needs any assistance. If they don´t want any help, there is not much we can do. We can`t work against the school`s wishes, can we?"

"Heather is right, if the school blocks us, we don`t stand a chance. I mean, think about the practicalities of this: if we are to help the school kids, we need to go to the school. That`s where the kids are and that`s where there is a certain room capacity to do anything, or am I jumping the gun here?" Tina looked a little doubtful. She wasn`t used to these kinds of discussions and in her heart of hearts, she was a first-class procrastinator. If they went to the school first, any decisions would naturally have to be put off till after that meeting.

Connor sat there, head sunk. "Call it cold feet if you like, but I have my reservations about this whole thing. There is no way I can find time to do anything in the way of helping kids before school. My morning shifts start at 6.30 am. This is completely illusionary. We have to back off before we go too far."

Janice stood up, checked orders for the next round and left the table to go to the bar.

"Just you listen to me, young man. I asked you straight out at the beginning of the evening, whether you were taking this seriously or not. You said you were. You said you were committed. So, don`t come this, oh, I`m getting cold feet with us now. That`s not on!"

Tina was getting worried. "Back off, Lavinia, Connor is not one of your children. You can`t speak to him like that."

"I can, and I will. We are either all in or all out. That is the way I see it. No changing of minds. We need to be able to count on all the others. ALL the others."

Janice returned with the drinks to find a strange atmosphere at the table. She placed the drinks in front of each respective person and said, "Cheers."

No-one replied, but everyone drank a sip.

It was Connor who broke the silence. "Lavinia is right. I`m sorry. I didn`t really mean I no longer want to do this, but I have to point out that I can`t do a morning shift at school when I have a morning shift at work."

"So, we define who can do what, and when, and how often." Heather was in her element, she loved organising. "But not yet – first, we check with the school and see what is necessary. Connor, you call the school and make an appointment with the headmistress. You are pre-destined for such tasks." She smiled warmly at him, smiled at the group, one after the other and took another sip of her lemonade-and–lime. The atmosphere cleared.

Lavinia suddenly remembered something that her daughter had said when they were discussing this over Sunday dinner. "Chelsey said that there is some cereal company that has a project called 'School Breakfast' or something like that. I don't know any details but it can do no harm to follow it up. I'll find out before we meet next week."

"You'll come with me, though, will you?" asked Connor. He was deeply disturbed by the daunting proposition of being the group's spokesperson at the school.

"Of course, I will. If the appointment is after 4.30, I have absolutely no problem with it. If you make one during the school day, please check back with me first, as then I have to ensure I can get time off."

There was now an air of optimism around the table. Even Andrew could see that there was a slight possibility that they could get something moving although he was not yet completely convinced that it really was any of their business.

Janice, for her part, was more worried that she may face some sort of consequences at the office. She was already putting her side of the story together should anyone question her about the "project."After all, it was a charitable venture. What could they really have against it? Other than the fact that she worked for the education authority and they were doing nothing. Would someone put two and two together and decide she was contriving behind her employer's back? It suddenly hit her that she had never actually ever stood up for any principle before. Never seen, or heard, something she considered immoral, illegal, or purely ethically wrong, and set about to change it. And here they were – the Six Pack - ready to embark on a project to feed hungry children in the town. Well, maybe not exactly FEED them, just give them some breakfast, and maybe not all the hungry children in town, just one class in one of the primary schools.

It was a start, wasn't it?

"Can we really single out one class for this project? Isn't that rather unfair?" she blurted out.

The group looked at her in astonishment. They were all still preoccupied with the subtleties of the project to date, not ready for more input.

This was unknown territory for them all, even the mothers among them had never lost a thought on the subject to-date. There, they were thrown in at the deep end – but all willing to show they could swim.

"Let's learn to walk before we try to run, shall we?" This was Andrew.

"It is a good point, though. We'll bear it in mind when we speak to the Headmistress."

They all drank up and left the pub to return to their stable, peaceful, orderly homes with their full fridges and pantries.

3/FIVE
Having the upper hand

Toby swore by his evening whisky now. Had it not been for his evening tipple last week, he would not have discovered the door to his escape from the apparent mess which Trish was obsessed on loading on him.

The very next morning he had called her and demanded – yes, demanded, not requested as had been his wont previously – a meeting.

She was reluctant, but agreed. She had asked what it was exactly that he wanted to discuss, had not all been said? Toby had his wits about him and said nothing of his real plan. He merely pointed out that he needed a little more info, nothing too extreme, but the quicker they talked it through, the quicker everything could be sorted. Was that not what both of them wanted?

They arranged a meeting for the day after, at 2 o`clock, in town, but not in the pub.

It, therefore, came to pass that Trish arrived on her own for the meeting and was in good spirits as she was convinced her plan was working a treat and she was soon to have reached her goal. She smiled broadly at Toby as he walked into the café.

His heart melted. She was a good-looker. He used to be so proud to be seen walking around with her. He stopped these thoughts in their tracks – and his rational took over. He greeted her with a smile and a kiss on her right cheek.

"You`re looking good, Trish. Life treating you well, is it?"

"Can`t complain. And you?"

"Have seen better times, as you know."

"I`ve ordered you a coffee, white, with sugar. Just as you like it."

"I've taken to black now. And no sugar, either. You're going to have to change the order, I'm afraid."

This was but the first surprise he had in store for her today.

The coffee arrived, and Toby braced himself to land the next blow.

Trish was completely oblivious to what was about to come. "Have you got everything settled then? Is that what you want to tell me in person?"

"Yes. I have everything settled in my mind. I am quite clear about the route we should take. Are you not having any cake today?"

"No, I have just come from lunch. I'm not that hungry. But you order some, if you want. Don't mind me."

Toby called over the waitress and ordered some apple pie with cream. He had all the time in the world. He smiled at Trish and looked around the café. It wasn't busy yet, the lunch crowd had left, and the afternoon crowd had not arrived.

"Shall I make an appointment with my lawyer, then? We can get everything sorted quite quickly, can't we?" asked Trish, after a while

"Why exactly should I need to meet with your lawyer?"

"Well, he has the agreement written up. If we meet there, it will speed up the process. You can sign there and then. Done."

"It doesn't work like that, Trish."

Trish looked quite taken aback.

The cake arrived, and he thanked the young woman with an exaggerated smile. He was quite enjoying this.

"I don't get you. We're talking about a financial agreement. Heavens, Toby. Even you can't be that stupid – haven't you understood what I have been saying?"

"Oh, I have been understanding quite well what you have been saying. I have looked through the papers numerous times and read – and understood - every line."

"So, why not sign them at the lawyer's office, then? Do you want to alter some of the clauses?"

"No, no, I don't."

"Right, fine. What do you want? Will you send them to him by post, or what?" "No, I don't think so."

"For goodness sake, Toby. Stop fooling around. When are you going to sign the papers and how will you get them to my lawyer?"

"I don't intend to have any contact with your so-called lawyer, at all."

"How will we manage this, then? And, what do you mean, so-called lawyer?"

"I don't intend to sign the papers, Trish."

"What?" Trish looked forlorn. She had no idea what to say. She hadn't been prepared for this. "What do you mean?"

"I want a divorce."

"What? You haven't spoken about a divorce before. Why now?"

"Because I have decided that is what I want."

"I need to go to the toilet," She stood up and left the table in the direction of the women's toilets, returned to pick up her mobile phone and then walked away, defiantly.

Toby tucked into what was left of his cake. This was going just grand, he thought.

Trish returned with an entirely different look on her face. She smiled at Toby, a deep, warm and almost affectionate smile. As she walked past him, she kissed the back of his head and played gently with his right ear.

She sat down and leant forward over the table, ensuring her cleavage was in full view.

"Don`t even think about it," said Toby. "I`m not falling for it."

"Don`t know what you mean."

"Yes, you do. And no, I`m not interested."

"How can you be so, so, so…. come on Toby. Let`s go home and talk about it there. It is so public here."

"I like it here. And, I like it public. There is no more "private" where we two are concerned. My mind is made up, Trish. You have gone a step too far and I am pulling the plug."

Trish looked like a schoolgirl who had been caught behind the bike shed.

"I don`t want a divorce. Things are not that bad between us, are they?"

"Yes, they are."

"I can`t afford a divorce," she heard herself muttering.

"Not my problem. I will get myself a lawyer and you will be dealing with him from now on. As soon as I have decided which one I will take, he will be in contact with you. Good-bye, Trish. Have a nice day."

He left her to pay the bill.

3/SIX
So many locks, not enough keys

Toby had been in a particularly good mood all week and was especially happy today as Rachel was coming in. Okay, it was to help out at the bar, but it meant extra time with her, which he relished. The college lads were both off on some trip, and so couldn`t come in, and Sadie and Cath were both allocated in the restaurant. The law firm on Trent Avenue was having a going-away party for one of their assistants and had booked the whole restaurant. That meant it was him and Rachel on "Smoke Room" duty.

It used to be called the Public Bar, was then changed to Smoke Room by his predecessor, and Toby had kept the name on even though no-one was allowed to actually smoke in there. Smokers had to leave via the rear door and take their place out in the courtyard which was between the main pub building and the former outhouses. It was cosy enough for a five-minute fag, but uncomfortable enough to ensure they all came back in again quickly and didn`t stand out there hugging half-a-pint for ages.

In the bay window stood the Britannia table in all its glory, and, as it was Wednesday, the Six Pack would take their place there by six o`clock. He placed the "reserved" card there in plenty of time, just to make sure it remained free for them. He liked them, all six of them. And ever since he had gone with five members of the group to cheer Janice at her wedding, there had been an increased bond. This bond was intensified by the fact that (his) Rachel had been the initial kick-starter of the group, without actually knowing it. They had all done a cookery class with her and had been meeting here ever since. He always looked forward to Wednesdays.

Whilst still reminiscing, the door opened and in walked Andrew and Tina. What a nice couple they made. They were closely followed by Lavinia and Janice, two very different personalities but nice enough in their own special ways.

They all took their places at the table and Andrew checked the drinks order. He walked over to the bar to order. "Not waiting for the others, then?" asked Toby.

"They may be a little late today. They're at a meeting at the school."

Toby looked puzzled. "If you have time, come over, and we'll tell you about it."

"Okay, I'll do that as soon as Rachel is here. You've certainly got me curious."

"In the meantime, we'll have a beer, a G&T, a lager-and-lime, and a lemonade-and-lime."

Toby looked puzzled again – this didn't quite fit the pattern – he said nothing, though, just served the drinks.

"Toby is curious to know what's going on. I told him he could come over. That's okay, isn't it?"

"Sure. We're not on any clandestine adventure, are we?"

"Can't wait to hear what Connor and Heather have to say about the meeting with the school headmistress."

Janice stood up, looked at the others and excused herself. By the time she got back to the table, Connor and Heather had arrived and were getting their drinks from the bar. She smiled at them and walked over to the table.

"Have they said anything yet? Did I miss something?"

"No. Not yet. They are keeping us on tenterhooks," said Tina, as if in jest but actually dying to know if they were to continue with this project or not.

"Right, cheers!" said Connor and gestured to Heather to take on the task of recalling all they had learnt.

She willingly accepted, "The Headmistress, a Ms Fairwell, was pleasant enough," she paused and took a sip of her lemonade-and-lime. "Listened to what we had to say and praised Connor`s Lucy to heaven and back. She explained that they were fully aware of the extensive problem which is prevalent in the school, on all year levels. Year 3 is a particular problem as the free school meals for all stop. Those families on benefits can apply for further free meals for their children, some do, some don`t – for a variety of reasons. Some parents give their children money for them to pick up a snack, but then they go and buy crisps, sweets and the like instead. A lot of the parents on the estate work shifts, meaning that some children leave in the morning without having had any parents around at breakfast time. The school has tried to get a breakfast club going, but that it failed miserably due to a lack of support by parents as volunteers to help out."

"You mean even the parents aren`t interested in helping get their kids fed – even for free? This is hard to digest." Andrew was quite disgusted. As a student, he had often enough been hard up and more than low on cash, but if he had had kids, then, he wouldn`t have made them go without food.

Heather pushed on, "It seems a little more complicated than that. It is a time thing. They are also having great problems with punctuality – and here it seems the parents are more the problem than the children. So, they have some parents who are already at work, and others who are still in bed when the kids go off to school. Neither groups can, or are willing, to help out. Let`s not forget we are looking at a shift between 7.30 and 8.45 am. It wouldn`t be an easy shift to fill off this table either, would it? We must stay fair."

"Did she give you the impression that they would welcome help?" Janice wanted to know, "Well, in one way, yes. However, she did make it quite clear that she didn`t think that it would be feasible. Quite apart from finding sponsors for the project, which would be difficult enough, we would need to have volunteers to help out – at least two every day, if not three – she made it clear that we couldn`t possibly just offer it to only one class, so as you foresaw last week, it would have to be offered to the whole school. She then also reminded us that all volunteers would need a DBS check, which costs around 18 pounds. It was all quite disheartening, really."

"We did ask what the school policy on fresh fruit was, and she explained that they have donations of fresh fruit in the school, but that is distributed to the younger children," Connor thought it was time he participated in the conversation. "We could easily extend that without getting into any problematic situations regarding potential allergy issues. That was what she said. Apparently, there are so many children nowadays with nut allergies and/or lactose and gluten intolerances, it seems like quite a nightmare."

"Did she make any constructive suggestions as to how we could help, other than upping the fresh fruit delivery?" Lavinia asked "As I see it, we are facing a battle which we, most likely, cannot win. There are simply too many obstacles. As they say, too many locks and not enough keys."

"We can`t just give up before we`ve really tried, though, can we? Connor, how does this all feel to you?"

"To be honest, Tina, I feel quite down. I`m really sorry I have dragged you all in on this. It was so stupid of me to make such a promise in the first place. It seems, purely and simply, that I have bitten off more than I can chew."

At that moment, Toby appeared behind them. He pulled up a chair from the neighbouring table and placed it between Tina and Andrew. After sitting down, he asked, "So, what`s the big adventure, then?"

"It`s been pulled to a stop before it even got properly started, I`m afraid," explained Andrew, who really was quite relieved.

"How so? What were you planning?"

It was left to Connor to explain everything to Toby from the start to the current apparent end. Toby listened intently, shifted every so often on his chair, was obviously interested in the project and visibly uneasy when it became clear that the hindrances were going to be too big to be able to do anything to help. When Connor was finished, he stood up.

"Shall I go get you all your next round? This could take a while."

Janice jumped up, "It`s my round. I`ll come and help you," she said. She greeted Rachel when they got to the counter. She hadn`t seen her since the day that she had got married, and so she felt she would like to thank her once again in person for being there. It had been such a wonderful surprise to find them all waiting outside the building when she came out with her husband, Tim.

Toby got the drinks, and Janice reminded him that she was on lemonade-and-lime today, so he should skip the white wine, please. He did.

They returned to the table, and both sat down again. Toby began, "First of all, I want to say how great what you are attempting to do is. Chapeau! There is one thing that I think maybe you …." He stopped in his tracks as he noticed that the whole group were distracted. Something was going on behind his back which had attracted their attention. Then he heard the voice, he would recognise it anywhere. He also recognised the pitch – she always spoke in that pitch when she was drunk. What the hell was she doing here?

Toby turned around and got out of the chair and walked swiftly over to the bar. There was Trish standing behind the bar, pouring herself a drink of red wine. There was defiance in her stance. She had obviously already told Rachel that she was having no objection from her. Who the hell was she anyway?

"What are you doing here, Trish?" Toby asked as politely as he could. "You have no right to be behind the bar, and certainly no right to be helping yourself to drinks."

"She wouldn`t serve me - refused to serve me! Thinks I`ve had enough already, Mrs High-and-Mighty, over there."

"Trish, come around here, to this side of the bar – where you belong."

"This is my home, forgotten? I have as much right – no more right - than anyone else I know."

"Trish, you gave all this up of your own free will. Now, come around to the other side of the bar."

"No, I won't. I don't need anyone to serve me here. I can get my own drink, and that is what I am doing. Just you leave me alone. Who is this woman, anyway? I don't know her. Where are Sadie and Cath?"

Toby recognised all the signs. Trish was on the warpath, was aching for a fight. He walked around to the other side of the bar and took the glass of wine away from her "Enough, Trish. Please leave." Trish stamped her foot and grabbed another wine glass from the counter. She slammed it down onto surface as she shouted, "Don't you talk to me like that!" The glass smashed into small pieces, and as she banged her palm down to accentuate what she was saying, "I'm not one of your drunken bar guests, you know" She looked at her hand, it was already bleeding quite readily. "See what you've done!"

Rachel stepped towards her. "I'll get the first aid box, we'll have to see to that quickly."

"Don't you come near me," she spat at Rachel with a venom which was palpable.

Toby could see the malice in Trish's eyes. He knew that this was not going to end well. He pressed the red button, which was located on the back counter, and within seconds, felt the vibration of the phone call in his pocket. If he didn't answer and give the code word, the police would be notified, and they would be here within ten minutes.

Rachel took a deep breath. "You need help," she said calmly.

"Not from the likes of you, I don't." With this, Trish swung her right arm back and, if it had not been for Toby would have slapped Rachel on the cheek.

Toby held Trish's wrist firmly. There were small splinters of glass still in her hand. If she had really slapped Rachel's face, Lord knows what would have resulted.

He was more than just angry. He was filled with an emotion that he had considered long gone from his repertoire. It was pure disgust, coupled with unadulterated hatred.

The once-time lovers stood there staring at each other, neither moving. Trish stunned, and Toby determined to keep control of this woman until the police arrived. They didn't take long to appear. They must have been nearby when they got the call to go to an incident at the Woolpack pub.

"Ease off, you two," the younger of the two officers said, as he stepped behind the bar. "What the hell is going on here?" He saw the trail of blood from where the glass was still lying, smashed on the counter and looked at the drops of blood coming from Trish's hand.

"I'll get the first aid box," said Rachel and left without awaiting an answer.

"Do you want to press charges, Sir?" The second officer asked Toby, "If so, we can't let anyone leave the pub until we have their statements."

"Yes. I do, officer."

Trish looked shocked

"And I want to get a restraining order to ensure she doesn't get the opportunity to do anything like this again."

Rachel returned with some tweezers and the first aid box, but the officer said he had just called for an ambulance. It seems this incident was going to be the start of slightly more trouble than expected.

Toby wanted so much just to hold Rachel in his arms and let her know that she was safe, that he would ensure Trish came nowhere near her in the future, but he decided maybe that might just pour more oil on Trish's fire, so he simply smiled as lovingly as he could and asked Rachel to go over to the restaurant bar and ask one of the guests to come over. Anyone of them would do – he just wanted to have some lawyer present. The formalities could be dealt with later.

The ambulance arrived and dealt with Trish`s injured hand while the officers took statements from the pub guests still seated in the "Smoke Room." Rachel and Toby were to come to the police station the following morning and give their statements.

As Trish was led out of the building by the police officers, she turned to Toby and screeched, "You despicable creature. How can you do this to me? After all I have done for you!"

Toby merely smiled and said, "You disgusting creature. How can YOU and this to ME, after all I have done for you?" His newly-appointed lawyer placed his hand on Toby`s arm to indicate he should say no more.

With Trish finally out of sight, Toby turned around and walked towards Rachel. He gave her the hug she had not only been waiting for since the whole episode started, but that all the on-lookers thought she whole-heartedly deserved.

The first guests started to get up from their chairs. They had experienced enough for one evening. Toby – ever the good host – announced that he would throw a round for everyone. He would serve them all at their tables.

Rachel pulled beer after beer and poured wine and spirits till the room was full of customers drinking their favourite beverages.

At the Britannia table in the bay window, the Six Pack all felt emotionally exhausted, for they not only had been party to this intense scene between Toby and his ex but were also – some faster than others – beginning to face up to the fact that their project to feed the school children a good breakfast was proving itself to be a non-starter.

It had seemed a good idea, at first. Simply follow in the footsteps of Connor's Lucy, but all too soon, they were forced to accept that it was definitely not that easy. In fact, it was nigh-on impossible.

It seemed a unanimous decision, though not outwardly communicated – that no more would be said of the project today. Next week would bring another Wednesday and they could discuss further steps then.

They drank up and left after thanking Toby and wishing him well. "See you next week."

3/SEVEN
Marching on

Once they had locked up the pub, they headed up the stairs together and had nearly fallen over a bag which had been placed halfway up the stairs. One quick glance inside was enough for Toby to realise it was Trish`s. She had seemingly assumed she could/would be staying overnight. Toby threw it down the stairs. It landed on the stone floor of the entrance area with a thump.

Now, Toby lay in bed next to Rachel, holding her close, feeling the warmth of her body, stroking her soft skin, sensing the relief of the overcome danger, and perceiving a certain change in their relationship

Their love-making was passionate and fulfilling. Toby wouldn`t call it sex. Somehow, he didn`t feel that was the right word. It was so much more. They belonged to each other, and they shared a sensation when together that Toby thought couldn`t be topped. It was so intense and so consuming that Toby wished to class it mature. This was something special. He could not imagine that anyone else could possibly experience anything close to what they had together. On the one hand, they were both old enough to have a certain mastery born of previous sexual experiences and thus know not only what they wanted, but also what they could respectively give, and on the other, they had a young love which was vibrant in its lust.

At this moment in time, they were happy to be with each other, lie next to each other, and know the other was there, and out of harm`s way. The atmosphere was all-embracing. Words were not necessary.

However, Toby did eventually speak, he said, "I`m so sorry about Trish coming here this evening."

"Hardly your fault, is it? You didn`t know she was coming, did you?"

"Would I have asked you to come if I had anticipated anything like that?"

"Tomorrow, we will give our statements to the police. I can't see there will be a problem with banning her from here after that performance."

"Well, we have a lawyer now, don't we? What a stroke of luck that was! He can deal with Trish from now on. I'm thoroughly through with her."

"Is he coming to the station with us?"

"He said he'd meet us there – actually, what he said was, the team member who will be taking the case on, will meet us there."

"Are they expensive? Sounds it, if they have teams of lawyers."

"You know, even if they are, I have a feeling that anything that happens from now on will be cheaper for me with them than without them."

"We have a busy day ahead of us tomorrow. Sleep well."

"You, too."

And Toby did eventually sleep well. In spite of all that had happened, in spite of all the anger milling in his head, in spite of all the worries that his wife had been inflicting on him over the past months, he slept like a log.

Toby had found his peace with himself

As he floated away into the land of nod, pictures of his situation flashed up, his brainwave to actually openly articulate a divorce had been a game-changer. How good it felt to finally appreciate her actions for what they were. Now so perfectly obvious that she had no intention of getting a divorce with a one-off payment, what she had wanted was a never-ending flow of maintenance money keeping her afloat in sunny Spain. How stimulating it had been as he had shocked her into reality with his stance at the café. She was definitely struggling with this reality. Once again, he saw her standing behind the bar, with that evil look in her eye, an action replay of the scene, resurrection of her performance, which he knew would help his case immeasurably. Toby relived it all in his mind's eye and was calmed by the thought of how well-documented and witnessed everything had been. Brilliant. He couldn't have staged it better. She wouldn't have a leg to stand on in court. His final thoughts of the day brought a smile to his face, which remained there long after he had entered the realm of slumber.

Refreshed, he awoke the next morning. Rachel, still sound asleep next to him. He looked at her and felt a surge in his breast. This was his love.

Dawn had broken, he could actually hear birds chirping outside. Was this heaven? No, it wasn't. A jolt back to reality - he had things to do, matters to be dealt with. He hadn't spoken about any financial aspect of the case with the lawyer. That would be one of the tasks for today. No matter, he had come to realise that anything would be cheaper than what Trish had originally demanded of him; on the assumption that he wouldn't take a lawyer. It did hurt a little to acknowledge that she knew him so well, knew he would resist the expense of a lawyer. But, things were different now

Not only was he seeing things clearly for what they were - he had Rachel. She was just what he needed. He loved her.

He was going to have to tell her everything now. It would not come easy to him, especially as he would have to admit that he had been keeping details from her, but she would understand. She was just perfect. She was not only his lover, she was his friend. Gone was the superficiality which Trish had personified, and in its place was an overwhelming intensity of abiding companionship, trust, and love.

The only thought that was still bothering him was that banning Trish from the pub was not going to be enough. He wanted, no, he needed, a restraining order. He had to keep Rachel safe, and as far as he could see, this was part of the way forward. However, he found peace in the thought that, as of now, someone professional would be dealing with his case. It was definitely the right thing to do. He knew his hand had been forced but was quite willing to accept that it was for the better. For all concerned.

Except for Trish, maybe, but what the hell did he care?

3/EIGHT
When you can't see the wood for trees

What a week that had been. Toby's feet had hardly touched the floor. Thursday had seen him and Rachel at the police station making their statement. The lawyer who was representing them, Jennifer Mulligan, was in her forties and had made a very good impression on them both. As far as they could judge, she certainly knew how to deal with the police. By 12 noon, they had not only decided on but also issued an "injunction without notice" that Trish could not come near the pub. This took effect immediately. Unfortunately, it was only effective for five days, but both Jennifer and the police felt it would definitely speed up the process of a restraining order. With some luck, this could be delivered by the beginning of the following week, and Jennifer knew which strings to pull.

Rachel was remarkably calm throughout and had even found an amusing aspect in the whole affair. She had called the school to let them know that she would not be able to come in for lessons on Thursday; she had explained that she had to go to the police station as she had been involved in a pub brawl the evening before. The school secretary didn't believe a word and had passed the call on to the deputy head, who also thought she was pulling his leg. Rachel insisted this was the truth, and a good laugh was had by all.

Friday found Toby at the lawyer's offices on Trent Avenue. He had an appointment with Jennifer to sign all the necessary papers giving her power to act in his name, and to discuss the details of the divorce. At first, he was slightly shocked when he was told that the solicitor's fee for the restraining order alone would be 2,000 pounds, payable in advance. Then he reconsidered; this was nothing compared to the peace of mind it would give him. Furthermore, it gained the insight that he was right in thinking that, in spite of the now inevitable lawyer's fees, he would get a much better divorce deal and would probably come out better, financially speaking, than without them.

Saturday and Sunday had been very busy days at the "Woolpack." If he hadn`t known better, he could have been tempted to believe that there was a certain aura of curiosity amongst the guests. Everyone had heard about the "brawl," and the majority wanted to be able to give their piece of info when conversation turned to it at work next week. There is nothing like a good pub fight to attract business, thought Toby. He hesitated to consider it as a viable strategy for the future, though.

Monday arrived, and Toby asked his "Man Friday" Jack to take Trish`s overnight bag to the contract address which he had received from the police. He had completely forgotten about it and really didn`t want to go himself. Jack returned with news that it was actually Trish`s lawyer`s home.

"I knew it all along!" said Toby. "Lover-cum-lawyer, right down Trish`s street," Jack said he was an obnoxious bugger and had been darn-right rude to him. "He was lucky I didn`t punch him on the nose for what he was saying about you, and the pub, and all of us who work here."

Then Jack had asked Toby for a moment of his time – as he had undoubtedly collected some brownie points by taking the bag over, he had something he wanted to ask. It turned out that Jack and the elder of the two permanent barmaids had been dating for a good six months, and Jack wanted to know if it was OK with Toby if she moved in with him and if it would mean an increase in the rent. Jack lived in the living quarters in the old shepherd`s outbuilding behind the main pub building. The rooms had been renovated for Jack to move in and were cosy and large enough for two. Toby was thrilled to hear the news and congratulated Jack on his good taste in women.

He had no problem with Cath moving in and if they should find that the place was maybe too small for the two of them, then one could consider adjoining the two rooms on the second floor. Jack didn`t want to jump the gun here, he was presently content with Cath and the space they had. Let`s take things one step at a time, he had said.

Toby was left flabbergasted. How on earth could he have missed this? How in God`s name had he not seen the signs? How had they managed to keep this from him? He had an antenna for these things – at least, he used to have. He knew Jack always kept his cards close to his chest. That was what he liked about him, but how had he missed seeing the romance evolving in front of his eyes? The answer was obvious: it had not been in front is his eyes. It had been behind his back; they had kept it a secret. Well, what do you know? Another facette of Jack, he could keep secrets, too. How lucky he was to have him around. It struck him that he had been so preoccupied with his own misfortune (i.e. Trish) that he had neglected his surroundings. Neglected to sense changes happening around him, and these were positive changes! It would have done him a world of good to have had something to be happy about. *Just goes to show*, he thought, *once you`re in a pickle, you can`t see the wood for trees.*

Tuesday brought the restraining order – Jennifer had been good to her word. How she had done it, no -one knew. Toby was more than satisfied with how things were turning out. He walked around with a constant smile on his face – even though this was his office work day!

Rachel had been staying with him since the episode with Trish. She was at school all day but spent the evenings with him and the weekend, of course. It was then she had calmly initiated her own campaign to tidy up Toby`s flat. Nothing too elaborate, dusting, re-arranging, throwing away old magazines, that sort of thing, although she had bought a few plants which made the snug look much more cosy. Toby wasn`t bothered by this. He felt she was actually turning the place into a home.

And now, there were to be two happy couples under the roof of the Woolpack. What an invigorating thought.

Then came the next revelation: Tuesday evening, Sadie had arranged with Cath to swap shifts and was taking the evening off. She had been on lunchtime duty and had stayed on a while longer. Toby thought it was to chat with Cath about her moving in, but it turned out this was not the reason. She was being picked up at 4 pm by her date. The date turned out to be none other than Connor! Toby stood aghast for a second when he saw Connor arrive and kiss Sadie quite passionately on the lips as a greeting. He hadn't noticed this, either! What was wrong with him? "Just goes to show," he thought, for the second time in under 6 hours "Once you're in a pickle …." Cath was later to tell him that the two had been seeing each other for almost as long as she and Jack. It seemed quite serious.

Now, it was Wednesday again already. He placed the "reserved" card on the table, as always and placed himself behind the bar, intent on planning his speech for the Six Pack. He had an idea which could get them out of the dilemma which they had found themselves in last week. He just hoped they hadn't done anything in the meantime themselves and effectively called the whole operation off. He could have asked Connor the day before, but it didn't seem quite the right moment.

He had talked to Rachel about this plan, and she thought it was more than good. As a teacher herself, she knew of problems with children not eating breakfast, however, as she was in a comprehensive school, the reasons were maybe slightly more diverse. Naturally, there were also families with children in secondary school who were hard up, but, at least as far as her pupils were concerned, Rachel was convinced that the main problem lay with the teenagers themselves, who simply wanted to stay in bed longer in the morning. They certainly seemed to have money for, albeit unhealthy, snacks during break time. Until now, she had assumed this was not the case in primary schools, and at the end of the day, she was aware that something needed to be done.

Children, of all ages, cannot adequately concentrate when their stomachs are rumbling. Free school food, or at least highly subsidized school food, was something she could whole-heartedly support. She was right behind him!

He had not talked to her about the divorce yet, bar telling her that he was filing for one. No details had passed his lips, and certainly nothing about all the trials and tribulations that had kept him awake at night for so long. He knew it was pending, and the time was more than rife, but the internalising of such personal and emotional events was of long-standing and hard to shake off. Plus, he was afraid of how she would react to him, keeping this from her all this time. Who knows, it could turn out to be the acid test for their relationship. How could he have been so stupid as to not have talked to her about it from the start? Apart from anything else, it would have very probably meant less sleepless nights for him. She was always so calm, and so understanding, and to top it all, she produced answers. Deep down, he knew – she would be right behind him.

3/NINE
Softly, softly catchy monkey

Rachel sat in the staffroom, enjoying the peace. There were no other staff members around, it was mid-morning, and lessons were in full flow. Her Year eight history lesson had been cancelled as her class was out on a field trip, and surprisingly, she had not been given a stand-in to do. So, she sipped at her coffee and pondered the events which had so dramatically changed her hitherto very normal life. After the death of her husband, she had taken quite a while to adjust to life as it was to be from then on. She had stayed in the bungalow, which had been their home for more than twenty years. On the one hand, it gave her stability and a sense of security, yet on the other, it brought home to her every single day that she was now alone, without her beloved husband. She still had the two children, of course, although they were no longer children. They no longer lived at home, both away studying. One doing a BA, the other working on her PhD. They came home regularly, she couldn`t really complain.

Then along came Edmund who had asked her to do a course at the Community Centre – a cookery class. Somehow, he knew one of her greatest passions was cooking. He was looking for someone with a pedagogical background to run the course at the centre, but for reasons he had kept to himself, he didn`t want a domestic science, or a home economics teacher doing the course. He wanted it to be a communicative forum for the participants, showing the community that the centre was there for the whole community and not just young adults. It had been a success, as far as Rachel could see – in fact, the group still met every week for a round of drinks and a chat. She sincerely felt that it had been a good portion of her work that had brought them together, and it was a rewarding sight for her to see them sitting in the bay window at the Woolpack every Wednesday. Oh yes, the Woolpack. That was the element that had turned her life around.

Once the course at the Community Centre was finished, Edmond had asked her out a couple of times. At least, that is how she had interpreted it – out on a date. However, it turned out that this was not the case. He was merely grateful for her assistance. Edmund was actually not interested one iota in starting a relationship with her - or, indeed, with any woman.

Not so Toby, the landlord of the Woolpack. He had taken her out, wined and dined her. She felt a million dollars when she was with him. Whenever she thought of him, her heart felt warm, as if something inside were turning over. Who would have thought that this was possible?

A new love at her age – but then, she was not even 60, love knows no boundaries. They were in love as if they were teenagers and made love as if they were experienced lovers. It was heaven.

Well, it would be heaven if there were not a spanner in the works, Trish, Toby`s wife. She wasn`t really his wife, they were separated, albeit not legally – yet. She was quite a character. She was a lively good-looker and, as Rachel had experienced first-hand last week, one with an inclination towards aggressive behaviour. For the first time in her life, Rachel had been exposed to pub life at its worst.

The fact that Trish had almost slapped her in the face, with glass splinters in her hand had ruffled Rachel slightly but she was damned if she was going to show it. Neither to Toby (to whom she wished to prove her stoical character) nor to Trish (to whom she wished to prove her strength).

The evening itself had been relatively easy to bear, Toby was there and was a tower of strength. It had been the day after, when she had nipped home to pick up some extra clothes that had made her feel really uneasy. She had seen an unknown car parked on the other side of the street and had thought nothing of it – until she recognised who was sitting behind the wheel. It was Trish. As she opened the door to the bungalow, there was a note waiting for her demanding, in no uncertain terms, that she keep her hands (dirty mitts) off Toby.

The exact words no-one else would ever know – she had thrown the note in the bin. However, after considering all the events, she had made her mind up quickly – she would stay at the pub for a while. At least until the situation was legally settled.

At the police station she had been hesitant to apply for a restraining order against Trish but Toby had warned her not to take this whole thing too lightly. She knew now, he was absolutely right. She certainly didn`t feel safe alone in her house – not at the moment anyway and until the order was finalised by the judge, there wasn`t an awful lot she could do.

Should she tell Toby? No, maybe not. At least, not yet. He had so much on his plate, and she could handle it – living at the pub, what could happen? She did feel apprehensive about not sharing the information with him, but she was sure he would understand that she just wanted to shield him from the stress it would bring. The mere knowledge that Trish may be stalking her, and threatening her would very probably surmount in him doing something which would be let`s call it "disadvantageous" when the divorce proceedings started. She wasn`t going to be responsible for that. Didn`t bear thinking about, God knows what he would do. No, much better, keep this to myself. Decision made.

For now she was happy to be the live-in lady-friend of the most desirable publican in town. She had started to tidy the flat up a little, he wasn`t the most orderly of chaps, but made sure she hadn`t overdone it – didn`t want to provoke him in her first week there. He could get irritable if he felt he was being pushed into a corner he didn`t feel good in. Apart from that, he had a heart of gold and was always trying to please others, and help anyone who crossed his way. Always thinking of others – she loved him.

But could she imagine living in a flat above a pub for the rest of her life? The flat oozed with potential. There was no doubt about that. She could imagine all sorts of refurbishments they could … but stop. She was running ahead of herself. Let`s learn to walk together first, Toby and I, then we`ll try running.

I'll go and fetch some more stuff from the bungalow after school today – some decorative stuff, some books, some more plants, some crockery...

3/TEN
Grabbing the bull by the horns

Janice and Lavinia entered the pub and greeted Toby with a wave as they sat down at their table. This was novel, until now it had always been Connor who would arrive first, or maybe not, maybe Toby had missed that change, too. Not that it was important, but he was attempting to return to his old self and take note of what was happening around him, be the old Toby who everyone liked and could relate to. He owed it to himself, and not least to Rachel, to cast aside his pre-occupation with his past (i.e. Trish) and to focus on his present and his future here at the pub; a publican who is not aware of his immediate surroundings and does not heed the wishes of his regulars is not worth a tinker`s damn.

In walked Heather, followed closely by Andrew and Tina. The women walked straight over to the table, Andrew took a left and came to the bar. It was his turn to buy the round of drinks, so he decided to do it right off.

"The usual, please, Toby."

"Coming up! I`ll bring the drinks over to the table for you. I have something I would like to talk to you about." This part of the plan was, however, not to be. Toby would have to wait as Jack hadn`t come over from the other bar yet. "I`ll be over as soon as Jack gets here," he said as he placed the drinks down in front of the respective persons.

As his back was already turned away from her, he didn`t notice the look on Janice`s face when he placed her white wine in front of her. Heather did, She placed her left hand softly on Janice`s arm and smiled, then exchanged their drinks. Janice smiled gratefully.

"Well, cheers, everyone," said Tina, obviously in a good mood today, which could not be said for everyone. "I`d like to put the time till Toby gets back to good purpose. We`d - that is Andrew and I would," she paused for a nano-second, but it was enough for the group to start grinning, awaiting the announcement. "We would like to invite you all to a house-warming next Wednesday. We could cook together, for old times' sake. What do you say?"

"What would we cook?" Connor wanted to know, as if that would in any way alter his decision to attend, or not.

Andrew obliged with, "My dish was potato lasagne wrapped in bacon. It was supposed to impress the ladies, so how about we cook that?"

"Sounds good to me. I haven't tried that one since we cooked it in class – of course, I don't have to impress the ladies, do I?"

The three ladies agreed that they were willing to be impressed and even to help out in the kitchen. They were a little disappointed that the announcement had not been more of a romantic kind, but they could be patient, they had time.

It was a done deal. Toby was back, Jack had arrived and taken over the bar for him.

"What's on your chest, Toby?"

"I've been thinking," he started. "Thinking about Connor's dilemma." He looked at Connor straight in the eye. Connor looked right back, and shrugged his shoulders.

"So I fucked up, what's new?" Connor's nerves were on edge.

"What's this supposed to be, Toby?" Lavinia was worried this was about to turn nasty. She had never heard Connor speak in that tone of voice before.

Toby held his hands up in surrender. "Stop. We're on the wrong path, already. This is not an attack. This is the cavalry approach."

He waited for signs of acknowledgement from around the table before he continued, "I heard all about your project from you last week before we were so rudely interrupted – for which I humbly apologise once again." Yet another pause. Somehow, he didn't feel he had created quite the right atmosphere for what he wanted to suggest. He couldn't spend the whole evening sitting here with them, enough. So, soldier on he must. "Kids' breakfasts are vital. We, as we sit here we all appreciate that. Unfortunately, there are other members of society who do not see the necessity, or do not have the necessary funds to comply with this basic need. Although I can see this is a problem, and although I can acknowledge that Connor has a duty to fulfil his promise to a dying woman, I can also predict that more problems may arise if outsiders – and that is what you – we – are in this case trample into the rescue."

He was completely out of his depth now. He was not a good speaker and he didn't feel this was going well at all. However, when he looked at the faces around the table, he could see that he did have their attention. Their undivided attention. They waited for him to continue. Not a peep was to be heard.

"We don't have the financial capacity, the logistic capacity, the rooms, the volunteers to tackle this. Even if the parents of the school kids wanted to help out in the school, they, too, would need to submit DBSs. It is a number too big."

He paused again, a pregnant pause, for effect – which it did not fail to have.

"However, I also heard Heather say the Headmistress had implied that the problem was not new, not unusual and was very varied in its sources. The underlying problem being that, in the case of the class of Connor's Lucy, it was Year 3, and they no longer qualified for free school dinners. This, in turn, increases the problem immensely. Therefore, I say, THAT is the problem we need to grab by the horns."

"School dinners?" asked Lavinia

"Yes, the fact that as of Year three, the school children do not qualify for free school dinners anymore."

"How does that make our situation easier, Toby?" Andrew was genuinely puzzled.

"Because school dinners are dealt with by the schools. They already have the basic structure. They have the suppliers, the canteens, the dinner staff …" he didn`t get any further; he was interrupted by Janice.

"But not the cash, Toby."

"So, that`s what we need to change," Toby beamed.

"You mean, we should lobby our town councillors, or what?"

"My suggestion would be we start a campaign where people donate money to finance free school meals for primary school children in the town."

"Toby, are you aware of how many primary school kids there are in the town?" asked Lavinia, "or even how many primary schools?"

"I admit I do not. But does that matter at this stage? The longest journey starts with a single step. We start with Lucy`s school, and specifically Year 3, and see how far we get."

Andrew was curious to know, "Connor, would such a project suffice to fulfil your promise?"

"I guess so. At least, I would feel happy with it. We would be doing something to help the kids, wouldn`t we? And, as has already been said, we can`t work from inside the school ourselves like Lucy could, can we?"

Toby signalled to Jack to bring over a further round of drinks.

"It would have to be official," Tina, ever thinking finances, "We would need a bank account specifically for the donations."

"And we need to get the word out. We can`t go knocking on doors, can we?" If Tina was in on it, Andrew was, as well.

Heather was still slightly wary of the idea. "Not quite what we set out to do, is it?"

Janice stepped in. "Better than standing at the school entrance every morning handing the kids a muesli bar and a drink of milk if you ask me."

"And that, my friends, is what we were heading for before Toby came up with this idea." Lavinia agreed, in principle, "Someone needs to get the ball rolling, in some way, just how I am still contemplating. How far have you spread your ideas, Toby?"

"To date, as far as Rachel, which, to my mind, is a very good start. She has contacts with the local press. If we can get the press in on it, we`re half-way there."

"Make that quarter - at best," said Janice. "But, yes. A very good start."

"Rachel reckons she could have them on board within the week."

"Do they write the articles themselves, or would we need to do it?"

"As far as I understand, Rachel would call them, explain what we want to do, they come over, interview the spokesperson and take a photo, and Bob`s your uncle."

"We don`t have a spokesperson," Connor was really quick to throw this remark in

"We have an initiator – that would be you, Connor," Andrew, also very quick off the mark.

"I can`t possibly do it. I am singularly the least appropriate person to take on that role. Anyway, the initiator is actually Lucy, isn`t it?"

"Well, she can hardly be our spokesperson, can she?" Janice, always ready with a negative punch

Heather had a suggestion, "Toby, we`re on the right track, at last. You are brilliant. We should start this in her name, we do it for her. Connor keeps his promise. We focus on her class, her school – probably have to extend it to the complete Year 3, otherwise, we`ll run into problems with Ms Fairwell – but basically carry on with what she was doing. Okay, slightly altered – she gave them breakfast, and we give them lunch. She can't do anything more, we can."

"And we can start before she dies," this could only be Janice.

"Janice, please. You're right, of course, but there's no need to be so, so blunt," Lavinia was of the opinion that the press chap would definitely do a better job of advertising the campaign than they would and that they should get him on board as soon as possible.

"But not too soon. We need to take things a step at a time. I'll wait for your word and only then get Rachel to move on it," Toby interjected.

"I think this is all sounding really good. I'll talk to her tomorrow – if possible. We can't use her name without her consent, obviously. I'll tell her what we want to do and see if I can get her okay. If she says she's behind us – I say, we go for it."

"So, who's the spokesperson? Connor?" Janice wanted to know.

"I thought I had made it clear that I can't possibly be a serious candidate for the post. Heather, how about you?"

"Well, to be honest, I don't think I'm up to it, either."

"If you're not, who is?" Janice again.

"This has become, and will most certainly become, even more of a group effort. No spokesperson – a whole group. We share the work, we share the responsibility, and we share the publicity. The Six Pack strikes!"

No-one would have imagined that Tina would be the group member to present such an idea. Just look how far she had come!

Connor felt quite proud of her – he always knew she had it in her to lead, not only to follow, and at a great distance, as that.

"Brilliant, Tina, lead us on!"

"What's Lucy's real name, Connor," asked Lavinia. "We can't call it the Lucy campaign, can we?

"I`ll let you know all next week – oh, we`re not here next week."

Toby looked surprised.

"We`re cooking at our place, a kind of house-warming," explained Tina, nodding in the direction of Andrew.

Heavens, thought Toby, *have I missed that, too?*

After much checking of mobile phones, hand diaries, and in-head-kept info, it was decided that they would meet at the Woolpack for an update and strategy meeting next Tuesday at 5pm.

3/ELEVEN
Success depends on backbone, not wishbone

Tuesday came, and when all had turned up, the meeting started.

"There were tears in her eyes," insisted Connor. "She was so touched by what we want to do. She was extremely worried about being pushed into the foreground, she didn`t want to be pitied or people giving money because they feel sorry for her. I told her they would be feeling more sorry for the poor kids and if the appeal were in her name, the connection with the school would be more apparent. I think I was able to convince her that it was for the good of the appeal. You know what, she even said she hadn`t thought I would really do anything. She had hoped I would, of course, but wasn´t completely sure and then had a bad conscience for burdening me with it."

"Well done, Connor," was all Heather could get out. "We have a dark horse in our midst!"

"That means we can go ahead?" asked Janice.

"Yep. She`s thrilled – Ellie MacGuiver - that`s her name. Miss Mac, they all call her at the school. She says she`s going to try and hang around for a bit to see how things kick off. I`m not putting my money on that, though."

"Right, so off we go, then! What is first on the agenda?"

Tina was ready, "Now we have the name of the appeal, 'The Miss Mac Appeal' I can fix an account up at my bank, no problem. It will have to be in a real person`s name, though. Shall I use mine? Is everyone okay with that?" Everyone nodded.

"We could make up a catchy slogan, maybe. That always helps, doesn`t it?" said Lavinia. "I think our press guy will be better at that, don't you? Or has anyone got any ideas?" Andrew did not have too much faith in the group as advertising experts.

Toby was in earshot of the conversation, although not sitting with them at the table. "Got it. I'll get Rachel on it right away and let you know when we have an appointment."

"We'll need some brochures, some flyers. Who can deal with that? And how quickly?"

Janice butted in "Hold your horses. We need a time schedule, first. Are we heading for next half term, or the beginning of the school year, or what?"

Connor intervened here. "If Ellie is to have any knowledge whatsoever of how the appeal is going, we have to get started quickly. She has no time to spare. In fact, she's on extra time already."

Tina, the organiser, had pen and paper at the ready: "So far I have: Tina: open bank account; Toby/Rachel: arrange meeting with press; Flyers question mark; buy collector's boxes: question mark; distribution of boxes: question mark; call companies for sponsorship: question mark"

"Stop, stop. Let's fill in the question marks as we go along, shall we? It would make things easier."

"I'll go and buy the collection boxes," Janice thought this would be the least visible role of the whole operation and was happiest with that.

"Okay, I'll create a draft for the flyers and have Ian check them with their marketing department. They'll know where is best to have them printed, as well."

Andrew thought he should be quick now, otherwise, he'd be left having to cold call companies for money. He certainly didn't fancy doing that. "I'll distribute the collection boxes."

All eyes were on Heather now. "Okay, okay, I'll send letters to local companies asking for a donation – Connor can help me. I'll write the letter. You dig up the addresses."

Thus, within minutes, the "Miss Mac Appeal" had taken shape.

Andrew was definitely on board but had never done anything remotely similar to this and thus needed info. "I don't want to be a party pooper, but we should discuss the finances a little, don't you think?"

"What do you mean by finances?"

"I mean our finances, getting the appeal on the road and the advertising, that sort of thing."

"We need to be organised, obviously," said Tina. "I don't mind being the treasurer of the committee."

"Would it be enough if I were responsible for keeping the minutes of each meeting we have?" asked Janice, still worried to be too publicly involved.

"Okay with me," answered Connor.

"I'm in with Heather on the selling side – we will choose the companies and contact them for a donation."

Heather agreed. "Yes, we'll have plenty to do on that score, won't we?"

"Well, in that case, does being responsible for distributing the collection boxes mean I have to choose the locations for them, as well?" Nods all round were answer enough.

"I think it goes without saying that the writing of the flyers is a mega task. The printing will not be cheap, but I'll see if I can get Ian's company to donate the costs. Would be great publicity for them."

Andrew was getting the hang of things.

"Okay, I'll see if I can get the DIY store to donate the money for the collection boxes – as well as placing them at the cash desks, of course."

"We still don't have a face for the campaign, do we? We need a head spokesperson. Someone well-known in the town, someone who is approachable, respectable, reliable, honest and hell, someone who has good contacts with the local press!" This was Connor speaking, but as he spoke more and more eyes focussed on the bar, behind which Toby stood and whose mouth was dropping by the second.

"Hold your horses, guys! I moved in to help out, not to be the mainstay of the whole operation."

"But you have to admit this would be the perfect headquarters, wouldn`t it? Plus, I`ll bring you the first collection box – yours will be the starter."

Toby was still hesitant.

"Without a spokesperson, we`re doomed to failure, that`s for sure," Janice was back in negative spheres.

"Yep, without someone to lead us, the whole thing descends into the realms of wishful thinking…" Lavinia, ever eager to help out, "Don`t let us down here, Toby."

"Don`t let Miss Mac down," said Connor. "Sounds like a slogan already, doesn`t it?" Heather could still hardly believe how fast things were progressing.

Toby pondered, juggled thoughts and decided, "Okay, here`s the deal. If Rachel will make a tandem with me, I`ll do it – we`ll do it. She would be so much better than me."

"Perfect – get her on board."

Janice had an appointment at the doctor`s. She needed to leave. Sorry to leave such a positive meeting, off she went.

Tina and Andrew were also in a hurry to get away, they still had to do the shopping for the meal next day. They said their good-byes, and left.

Connor was going to stay around for a while. Sadie was on duty in the restaurant bar, he would grab something to eat there.

Heather and Lavinia stayed seated. They would have a drink together and then go home.

3/TWELVE
Every picture tells a story

Connor arrived at Tina's house first and parked his car on the forecourt.

"Long time, no see!" Tina and Andrew were really quite nervous having the group around – it was such a step.

Janice's house was the only home that the group had ever been to. It was for her so-called "hen party." My god, what a house it was! This one here couldn't stand any comparison. Indeed, they were nervous what everyone would think. But they were, to a certain extent, proud of what they had achieved here. After all, they were mere housemates – sharing home space – and for that, it was really cosy, in fact, homely.

The doorbell rang again, it was Lavinia and Janice who had travelled together. That in itself was a godsend, only one car.

"Did you find a parking space easily?"

"Yes, no problem right outside."

Lavinia brushed past Andrew into the living area "Oh, how cosy," she exclaimed and sat down quickly on the armchair by the window, worried that there actually weren't enough chairs for all of them. Andrew and Tina exchanged glances, but smiled, that was Lavinia for you.

Andrew still had the door handle in his hand as Heather turned up. She placed her parcel down in the hallway and greeted them both warmly. It was so refreshing to see such a lovely couple settling down together. The sitting room area was at the back of the house and furnished with a three-seater couch and two armchairs in a shade of purple. There was a coffee table between with small dishes of salty snacks and peanuts on it. The television took up almost the whole wall to the right, obviously a much-used object in the house. On the wall to the left there were two large posters, one depicting Klimt's famous Kiss and the other an underwater scene, both framed in black.

Andrew was not used to playing host, but was determined to do well in his new post. He announced he would bring the drinks. Fortunately, he checked first. Janice was off-white wine and preferred a lemonade and lime. No-one thought this in any way strange, as she was probably the driver. The drinks were brought in on a tray and handed out. A toast was in order.

"Here's to the new home-owner and her home-sharer!" pronounced Connor.

Suddenly, Janice stood up. "I have something to tell you all before we start preparing the food, and you all start wondering about me," she paused, obviously feeling slightly self-conscious. "You see, Tim and I are ….." she paused again.

Oh no, everyone had the same thoughts. *Not so soon, they have only just got married, they can't be splitting up again!*

"We are expecting a baby."

The relief could be grabbed.

"Oh my God, congratulations!"

"Now all becomes clear."

"I knew it all along – ever since you started drinking lemonade three weeks ago!"

Tina was very happy for Janice, but did feel slightly put out that her moment in the sun was being "stolen." *This is my party*, she thought. The feeling didn't last long - truth be known, she was very happy for Janice. And, she was proud of what she and Andrew had here.

"Let's move into the kitchen. We've started to prepare the stuff."

They had indeed already peeled and grated the potatoes, and all the other ingredients were laid out on the working surface. The oven was already heated up – off to work, they all went! When they had decided that this should be this evening's dish, they had completely forgotten that it actually took 45 – 50 minutes to cook and had been a little worried as to how to pass the time. They shouldn't have worried at all. The group had plenty to talk about.

They all sat down at the dining table, which was situated in an extended part of the kitchen. Normally, there were only four chairs, but Tina had picked up two extra from her parents' house that morning. They looked slightly out of place, but no-one really cared. Cooking together had reminded them all of the experiences they had had during their cookery class with Rachel, and all were swimming in fond memories.

Once sat around the table, Tina announced that she had opened the account for the appeal and put in twenty pounds to get the ball rolling. Andrew beamed at her. She continued; she had also spoken to her manager at the bank. He was going to organise a donation from the main bank to the sum of 500 pounds. Andrew added that he too had been successful: he had bought 20 collection boxes, which had been paid for by the DIY store. William, his manager, was also checking with their headquarters whether they could give a donation, he had suggested 300 pounds. "We should have an answer by the end of next week."

It was Tina's turn to beam at him now. Janice said she had written up the minutes of the meeting yesterday and would send them out per email to everyone. She wanted to know if she should make notes today, as well. What, with so much news flying around? Lavinia was not to be left out here; she had written a draft text for the flyer and had it with her for everyone to have a look at. She handed out the copies and waited for some response. It didn't take long coming.

Connor didn't dare find fault as he hadn't really done anything yet. Heather was also rather quiet, as she, too, had not had time to start drafting the letter to the companies. Janice was happy someone else had written it and thought it was fine. Tina thought that it was maybe a little too long. Flyers have to be short and to the point- with more buzzwords than anything. If people have to read too much, they lose interest.

Andrew agreed; "Rather than explaining too much, we could concentrate on the fact that school dinners after Year Three are not free for all children. That was the crucial message to get across. The Education Authority <u>don`t</u> pay, and some parents <u>can`t</u>."

Tina and Andrew were obviously on one wavelength here, and it was contagious. Suddenly, the others were in the discussion and agreed with them. Less was definitely more when it came to flyers.

Plus, the slogan was still missing. They had to wait and see if the press guy would be of any help on that score. Lavinia was a bit peeved but got the message and promised to have another look at it and await the slogan before passing it to the marketing department in Ian`s company. She also committed to sending copies to the others via email before approving print. Oh, and Ian had committed to donating the cost of the printing. Connor was overwhelmed.

"Just wait till I tell Ellie about this. We have 820 pounds in the appeal before we have even really started. And no overheads to deal with to date. She`ll be thrilled. Plus, before I forget .." he practically giggled here.

"Toby called me. Rachel is in. We now officially have a tandem head to the appeal."

Heather laughed. "My God, what can go wrong?" Then, as an afterthought, "We should go and inform Ms Fairwell about these developments, don`t you think, Connor?"

"Yes, we should. Ellie told me that a school dinner would cost around 3 pounds per child per day and that there are around 190 school days in a school year. That amounts to around 570 pounds per child per academic year. Maybe I should check that. Also exactly how many pupils they have in Year 3 at the school. Whatever it may be, we should assume we will be needing in excess of 45 thousand."

"We shouldn´t get too excited. Let`s see what the press has to say about how they can help. It`s make or break there, I reckon. Did Toby mention anything about that?" smirking was always Janice`s patch. "Oh, yes. He said they were waiting for confirmation, but it may be possible on Saturday around lunchtime. How many of us can be there on Saturday around 1 o'clock? I've a shift, so I'm out."

The mothers' corner looked very dismal, with children at home, Saturday lunchtime was not a good time for press interviews. Tina and Andrew turned to each other and almost, just almost, held hands whilst looking each other in the eye. Could they make it? Yes, they could. Connor would let them know as soon as it was settled. The potato lasagne was ready to eat – and eat it they did. It was delicious. The healthy appetite that they all had, except Janice, who was rather off food in her present stage of pregnancy, ensured that the two oven dishes were completely emptied. As the meal drew to an end, Heather disappeared into the hall and returned with the package she had left there earlier. "We would like to thank you two both for the invitation and the lovely evening. This is for you both. May you make good use of it." As Tina unpacked the present, it became clear quite quickly what it was – the same present that they had given Janice at her hen party – a meat grinder. In remembrance of the "Minced meat cookery class" that had brought them all together in the first place. "We will make good use of it."

"Yes, we promise."

After the meal, they all had some cheese and biscuits and a coffee – except Janice, of course, and by 10 pm, everyone was ready to depart for home. This time they could all drive themselves, not like the last meal they had eaten together …… they had all needed taxis to get home from there. Andrew and Tina were left to clear the table, clean the kitchen, and generally tidy up. They did it with an ease that was astonishing. This was based on a mutual sense of pride and satisfaction, in the way the evening had gone, in the way they could interact, and in the way they felt for each other.

Once finished in the kitchen they went up the stairs to bed, hand-in-hand and completely in harmony.

What a picture – and, every picture tells a story.

3/THIRTEEN
No sooner said than done

James, the reporter from the *Town Chronicle,* couldn't make it on the Saturday – he was a local reporter, after all, and there was always so much going on at the weekends. He could not figure out how anyone at the newspaper could imagine he would have time on a Saturday. Monday late afternoon would be okay.

He duly arrived at the "Miss Mac Appeal" Headquarters, aka the Woolpack, at 5.00 pm and was pleased to see the "committee" already there. He didn't notice that Janice and Heather were missing, simply counted six and assumed it was the Six Pack. Must have had his head elsewhere. He should have noticed that this wasn't the same group he had interviewed after their cookery course at the Community Centre.

He gathered all the information, made what seemed never-ending notes in his laptop, and then sat back in his chair "Chapeau," he said. "I'll do what I can to help you."

Toby had some extra info for him, and wondered if it could be included. He wanted to initiate a sponsored run. He would put out a list at the bar and ask his regulars to participate. He hadn't actually done anything in this direction yet, though. Could it still be included? He would pull his socks up and get everything up and running (he enjoyed that pun, and laughed at himself) by the weekend.

"Sure. It will give some extra publicity. But when would the actual Sponsored Run be? We would need a set date."

Toby grabbed his phone and checked the diary. "How about in four weeks' time?"

"Okay. I'll add that info. They have to register personally here, I suppose?"

"Err, yes."

"Right. So, I'll call up the Headmistress and get her pitch on the whole idea, and that should complete the info. If you could give me a list of the places where the donation tins are, that could be added in an info box next to the article – along with the account number for donations."

Tina had the account number on a card in her handbag – she handed it over, and it was noted. Andrew admitted that he didn't have a list with him, but he could send it by email by – Thursday?

"Okay – fine. Then I'll have the article in the issue that comes out on Friday."

Andrew had something else on his mind "We don't have a catchy slogan yet. Do you think we need one?"

"Miss Mac Appeal is a good name. A slogan does go down well, though. Let's see, what did you say earlier about the parents not being able to pay and the town council not being willing to. Maybe we can work on that."

"I don't think we should necessarily point the finger of guilt at the education authority or the town council, do you? We're not in this for political reasons."

Lavinia felt she should tread softly in this area. Her husband had aspirations in this direction, which she couldn't ignore.

"Rather long for a slogan, anyway, don't you think?" Tina would have loved to help, but this was not her forte.

"How about *Please donate generously* (that is always somewhere on the blurb) followed by: *some don't, some can't. Will you?* Or, no – I've got it – *Free for Year Three. How about that?*"

"I knew the press could fix it! Perfect. Well, I think so, anyway."

And so did everyone else. Decided

At that very moment, the press photographer arrived. Late, as usual, but welcome, nonetheless.

He took his photos and names were noted. It was at this point that James realised that it was not the original Six Pack sitting before him. So, it was the Six Pack + Two running the appeal. Somehow, this had not been particularly well articulated, certainly not sufficiently. He had somehow got misled: it was the Six Pack as the original six cookery course participants, plus their teacher, plus her partner, the pub landlord – he would have to alter the text a little. Got to get the facts right.

He checked, "Can I call Toby your partner, Rach?"

The look Rachel and Toby gave each other deemed an answer unnecessary.

He jotted it down on his laptop.

3/FOURTEEN
Don`t count your chickens

Rachel was getting extremely worried. Every time she had gone home to check her plants and her post, there would be a note lying on the mat. A note from Trish. The wording was almost always the same, but nonetheless, each note seemed more aggressive. It was the mere repetitiveness that made it appear so. Trish was after her; Trish knew where she lived; Trish was not going away.

Rachel still hadn`t mentioned anything to Toby, had kept the fear and the anxiety locked away inside, afraid of what he might do if he knew. On the one hand, she should have been eased by the thought of his potential protection, on the other – which by far outweighed this – was the thought that he would do something rash.

Thus, as she sat in her front room pondering her options, she found herself weighing up what was important in her life.

Her children; definitely, but they were already leading lives of their own.

Her job; yes, but she was planning to retire soon.

Her garden; interesting as a hobby, but hard work and the garden was very big

Her home; hmm, it was very difficult living alone in the house where one had spent so long living together with someone – and, it also was too big for her on her own.

Her hobby; she could cook just about anywhere

Her boyfriend; yes, he was important. Was she ready to move in with him permanently?

She stumbled slightly here, for this question would have been a lot easier to answer if he had not lived in a flat above a pub. That was not what she had bargained for in later life.

It was his pub, he wouldn't be moving away from it in the near future. The flat had what one might call Olde-Worlde-Charm and loads of potential, but whatever one did, it would remain above a pub. They could have the whole of the upper floor, it was certainly big enough. There would not be huge structural changes needed, but then, whatever positive points she found, everything always came back to that one big main point – it was above a pub.

An idea was forming – was it feasible? Was it affordable?

She made herself a pot of tea, and made herself comfortable in the lounge and opened her computer.

A real estate website would be able to feed her with all the answers.

How much was her bungalow worth at present? It was a question she had never asked herself. It had never occurred to her that she should, could, or would sell up. She found plenty of comparable properties in the area and was able to make an educated guess at what she could make out of a sale.

Could she get a comfortable property in, or near a seaside resort, somewhere in England for the same price? Or maybe even cheaper? Where should she look?

She remembered that once a friend of hers had moved to Norfolk and swore it was the best move she had ever made. They had somehow lost contact over the years, but it was near somewhere near King's Lynn.

Rachel checked – she couldn't believe the prices. She could easily buy one!

The fun she had flipping through property photos made her lose all track of time.

It was going dark outside, and the phone rang. *Probably Toby wondering where I am*, she thought. But no, as she answered the phone, no-one said a word. Nothing. Silence.

Rachel drew the curtains as calmly as she could, inside, she was petrified. She called Toby, could he come over? They could go out for a meal, maybe? That was not possible, he was alone in the Smoke Room, but he was looking forward to her coming home soon.

He had called it "home."

Rachel got the whiskey out of the cupboard. She knew it wouldn`t necessarily help, but she did feel better even after that single first sip.

The telephone call had unnerved her, nothing like that had ever happened before, and now, with the whole episode with Trish still omnipresent in her mind, it was, quite frankly, scaring her.

To take her mind off the telephone call, and off Trish, she returned to her computer. In her mind, she was even more determined now to find a solution.

She clicked on "King`s Lynn" and lo-and-behold, just a few miles away from there, there it was – the perfect property. Just what she was looking for.

Was it the whiskey? No, she had only taken a couple of sips, but this really did look perfect. Sometimes, if things are meant to happen, they just do. Of this, she was sure. She read through the description, looked at the photos, checked on Google street maps and after 15 minutes, decided this was the – definitely the kind of – place she wanted to move to. She sent off an email, asking for a viewing appointment. At the weekend, if possible. Saturday morning would be perfect.

With that done, she closed her computer down, packed it into her bag and walked over to the telephone. She called a taxi. She would worry about getting to school tomorrow later. Toby could actually take her. That shouldn`t pose a problem, really.

Back at "home," in the flat above the pub, Rachel poured herself another whiskey. Toby would understand.

She needed to gather her courage, for she was going to tell him.

He hadn`t managed to get upstairs any earlier than normal even though Cath had come over to help in the Smoke Room, but up he came to the flat, eager to spend time with Rachel. He was certainly surprised to see that she was drinking whiskey, alone. That was a new one for him.

She offered him a glass, and he readily took it.

"I`ve decided to sell up," she said. Completely out of the blue, just like that. No introduction, no smooth talking, just pure information. It took Toby rather by surprise.

"That`s grand," he said. He hadn`t expected her to want to move in with him this quickly, what with all that was going on and the fact that he lived above the pub, but he had absolutely no objections. OK, maybe it would have been fairer to talk about it first, but heck, he was happy with this.

"I`ll be contacting an estate agent tomorrow, and they can deal with everything."

"You certainly don`t hang around when you`ve made up your mind, do you?"

"Why should I? Life is up for grabs, you know!"

"Any more surprises in store for me, then?" asked Toby, thinking he was being funny.

"Actually, yes."

"Oh, hit me with it," he thought he was in for a good night.

"I`ve decided I will retire at the end of the school year."

"That's great news. You really are full of it today, aren't you? Let's celebrate; I'll get Jack and Cath to step in, and we'll go out for a meal at the weekend."

"Ah yes, the weekend."

"Not another surprise, good grief, woman."

"I've found a bungalow in North Walsham which I would like to go and view. Would you come with me?"

"What? A bungalow? I don't follow."

"Yes, I sell up here and buy one in Norfolk. By the sea."

"And I come and visit?"

"No, silly, you come with me to view the bungalow. I've requested a viewing this weekend."

"I'm not sure I can make it this weekend." Toby was down, way down. This hadn't entered his head. She would up and leave him? He could come and visit every now and then? Who does she think she is?

"You just said you could get Cath and Jack to come in."

"Yes, that was when I thought we were celebrating."

"We can celebrate in Norfolk."

"And what exactly would we be celebrating?"

"Our new life together!" Rachel was getting more and more puzzled, how come he didn't think this was a good idea?

"Sure, Brilliant. Listen, it has been a long day. I'm off to bed. Sleep well."

Toby didn't sleep well. How could he have misunderstood all the signals? He was sure she wanted a stable, long-term relationship. Why, she had even admitted it to the bloody reporter from the *Town Chronicle*. Bloody women.

Rachel didn't sleep well, either. What the hell was wrong with Toby? She had been so sure he would love the idea of a cosy holiday home for them to escape to whenever they wanted. Away from the pub and away from the outside world – just the two of them. Obviously, the pub meant more to him than she had foreseen. Damn!

Breakfast next morning was a silent affair. Until Rachel decided she had had enough of it.

"This is ridiculous, Toby. I thought you would be thrilled at having a getaway place to go to. I didn't realise that the pub meant so much to you. I mean, I knew it means a lot, but I didn't realise that you can't leave it – even for a holiday."

"I don't want a holiday with you, I want a life with you."

"But that is what I want too."

"Then why move away? Stay here with me."

"That is also what I want. You don't get it, do you?"

"No, no, I don't. You're going to have to spell it out for me, Rach."

"I buy a house in a seaside resort for us to use as a getaway or a hideaway if you like. A place where we can go when we want to be alone, just the two of us."

"And the rest of the time?"

"The rest of the time I spend with you here, helping in the pub, creating a nest up here, a nest for us. We could have the whole storey – it could be lovely."

What a waste of a night together, thought Toby, and a similar thought ran through Rachel's mind.

3/FIFTEEN
Rest on your laurels

The article was printed in the weekend issue of the *Town Chronicle*, as promised by James. He was as good as his word – he certainly was behind them. All the relevant information was included, and quite a bit of background information, as well. Some of which even the Six Pack didn`t know. For example, just how much extra work and effort the teachers at the Woodford Estate Primary School put in every week to improve the well-being and education of their pupils. There was even a photo of Miss Mac, taken during a Sport`s Day while she was still teaching there. Their campaign had a face! They could not have wished for more support from this channel.

They all met for their weekly get-together at the Woolpack in particularly good moods. And with all good reason, the appeal was going extremely well. Much faster, and better than they had expected. It was becoming clear that there was a lot of work surrounding the appeal, which, if they were honest, they hadn`t really anticipated.

"Thanks for the swift feedback on the flyers, everyone," said Lavinia once they were all seated around their table with drinks in their hands. "The flyers are already spread around the town. I had Chelsey and George on the job yesterday after school. They weren`t thrilled at the task, but with a little gentle persuasion, off they went. I have the invoice from the printers for you, Tina. Has the donation from Ian`s company arrived on the account?"

"Yes, it landed on Monday. And since then, we've had quite a number of donations from citizens of the town. We stand at 3,240 pounds at the moment. And the donation from our bank HQ isn`t even included yet. I`m keeping a good tally on all bank movements, though. I`ll keep you all up-to-date via email. Every milestone will be documented, I promise."

"I've distributed the collection boxes all over town. The shops were really obliging. Only one shop owner said he didn't want anything to do with the appeal. Everyone else was all for it."

"Ellie is thrilled to bits. I showed her the article on Monday, and she cried and cried. Wishes us all the best and thanks us all for all our hard work. Heather can tell you more about the letter side."

"Oh yes, that is rolling. We sent out 25 letters on Monday morning to small firms with offices here in town and a further 16 to lawyers, doctors, and accountants. We won't be getting answers from them directly – so we'll just have to wait and see what Tina has to say about the response in the next few days and weeks."

"I'm adding all the incoming info into the minutes file on my computer. How often do you all want to have an update?"

"I don´t need it too often. Actually, the way I see it, it is more a kind of administrative backup that we can show we have been thorough and stuck to any rules. Or, what do the rest of you think?"

"Seems to sum it up."

With this, Toby arrived at the table. "Evening, all," he said, also obviously quite chuffed at the way the appeal was progressing.

"I just wanted to give you a rundown on how the Sponsored Walk is being received. Notice I am now calling it a sponsored WALK, not run as originally planned."

"Did you run into trouble calling it a run?" laughed Andrew.

"Some of the regulars thought it would be more appropriate if called a WALK," Toby explained. "We have 24 participants already, and they are busy collecting sponsors. All I need now are some volunteers to help out on the organisation day," he looked around, willing them to volunteer on the spot. It was not as easy as he had thought it would be. "Rachel is going to help out. What about you, Janice?"

"Okay. I'm in, but I can only do maybe 2-3 hours."

"Ah yes, in your condition ….. Tim bought a round to celebrate. Congratulations. Tim is participating, you know."

"Ian is, as well," Lavinia was quick to add, "so I'll do a couple of hours, too. I'll see if I can get Chelsey and George to help out, as well."

"Okay, okay, all this peer pressure! I'm in for a stint, maybe two hours? I'll talk to Jack and see if he would participate. When is the deadline for registering?"

"Just give us a call, Heather. I'll add him to the list any time. Andrew and Tina have already promised their help, so that only leaves you, Connor. How about it?"

"I have to check my shift first. But if I'm not working, I'll come along with Sadie – if you give her the time off," he grinned.

Toby grinned back and turned to return to his shift at the bar.

The drinks were already finished, so Heather stood up, checked the orders, and followed Toby to the bar to get the next round.

When she returned to the table, there was a strange feeling to be perceived. Something was amiss

"What's wrong?" she asked. "What have I missed?"

"Janice has just made a very important, and actually a very spot-on statement, at that."

Janice sighed a sigh of relief. She clearly had not known how her initiative was going to be received by the group.

"Oh come on. Tell me. Don't leave me in suspense!"

Janice thought it was only fair that she be the one to recount what was on the table. "I, well, you see, this is not easy, actually. I am completely behind what we are doing to help Connor in his venture, and I am more than completely behind the Six Pack in all we have done together and I appreciate, no... more than appreciate, what you all mean to me – what we all mean to each other. However ...," she paused.

The pause wasn`t for effect, it was because she knew it was right for her, but she didn`t want to force anything on anyone else.

The appeal is proving very time-consuming, and at the moment, I am not particularly... well, I am running at limit. I think I need to have a break. Not before the appeal is over, of course. I will see that through. But afterwards, well, when the baby arrives, I`ll be short of extra time, anyway, won`t I? Please, please don`t get me wrong here. I love our meetings, and I love our group. It is one of the best things that have ever happened to me, but I have to budget with my energy and my time now."

Heather smiled at Janice. She fully understood. Then she looked at Connor, who had said "spot-on" when he mentioned the statement Janice had made. "Do you feel the same, Connor?"

Connor couldn't look them in the eye. "Shit. You always ask such direct questions. But yes, I agree with every word that Janice just said. I am so, so grateful for how you all helped me when I made that promise to Ellie. I could never have even begun to keep my promise without you all. None of us knew just how much time we would have to invest. It is worth it, and I wouldn`t have missed this experience for anything, but we should be honest with each other. Meeting every week is great, but it brings its limitations. We are good together, and we should stay together. I will always be grateful for what you all have given me, and I feel rather guilty about putting such a strain on us all. Maybe we should simply fix a different kind of tact."

Heather smiled again. She had always had a soft spot for Connor, right from the start. "What do you think, Lavinia?"

"I wouldn`t have brought the subject up myself. But, hearing what both Connor and Janice have said, make me think, yes, perhaps we should re-think. I mean, before we flog the horse till it dies on its feet, we should re-consider. We will have plenty to do with each other over the next few weeks. No question about that. We all have our tasks and they all take up time – we'll definitely have contact. We don't need the Wednesday evenings on top, do we?"

"Before you ask, Heather, we agree. It's funny, but we were only talking about this yesterday evening at dinner. There is so much to do to keep the Appeal show on the road and make a success of it, that it is a strain on one's time meeting every Wednesday, as well. And anyway, we have the strength of the Appeal that will keep us together. Once it is over, we will probably all need some breathing space. I am more than grateful for all the group has done for me. The last thing I want is for us to split up. I guess that's why I think we should take a break once the Appeal is over. We need to refresh our bond, so to speak."

"Yes, that's right. Once the Appeal is over, we will need a break," Andrew nodded in agreement but still asked. "What do you say, Heather?"

"I completely agree. None of us knew what we were letting ourselves in for when we started this Appeal – and we are all committed to seeing it through. That is the main thing. No-one is backing out, with this discussion, we are simply ensuring that our relationship survives and has a future. I think it's super that we have the strength to do that. We should be proud of ourselves."

"Well, Ellie certainly is ..." said Connor, "And I am, too. Here's to friendship, honesty, and mutual understanding."

"And our sense of community..."

"However the Appeal ends, we have made a statement, have listened, helped, and done something to effect a change."

"Have proved ourselves - to ourselves and to others."

They drank to that, drank up, and all went home with a strong sense of well-being inside.

3/SIXTEEN
From Full house to Full Pack

Toby had always envied the Six Pack. From the very first time they had entered his pub for their first evening meeting after the cookery class, he had sensed a special type of togetherness and belonging. And it had made him envious. He had so much wanted to be part of the group. Had even for a while considered that he could be thankful to experience their group feeling and that it could wear off on him. He had always wanted a friendship like they had, but somehow had never quite had one. Comeraderie in the Army, yes, and there you had to rely on each other, unconditionally, but it didn`t seem like a friendship. And certainly not such enduring friendship as they seemed to enjoy. And look at them, they were such an odd group. Who would have thought that they would fit in together? It was Rachel who had done that. She had told him about their cookery class and how they had bonded - slowly, but surely and how proud she was to have been part of the process. She had been upset at first when they hadn`t included her in the weekly meetings, but just as Rachel did, she laughed it off. Well, there is no such thing as a Seven Pack, is there? And she certainly didn`t want to be a six plus one. She didn`t need them.

Now, they were using the pub as their headquarters for the Appeal, and he could watch them work together. He had now heard from them that they would not be meeting every Wednesday in the foreseeable future. They would meet when necessary to deal with Appeal matters. Once the Appeal was over, they intended to meet every month. On the first Wednesday of the month. They were so focussed, he was quite astonished.

He was doing his bit for the Appeal, and it was enriching. The Appeal was really going well, and most of the money they had envisaged had already been donated. His Sponsored Walk was going to be a good booster to the fund of that he was sure. It felt good to be part of it.

He was doing it all because he believed it was a good idea. And, it was very good publicity for the pub. He was also doing it because he wanted to belong – to them. How silly, he thought. I don`t need them.

He reflected on how stupid he was. How could he say he didn`t have good friends? What were Jack and Cath, and Sadie too, in fact. They were staff, colleagues maybe, but they were reliable and loyal. They were friends, they would be there for him if ever he needed them.

Furthermore, he had Rachel. You couldn`t get more loyal than her. She loved him, she was going to turn her life upside down for him. He loved her, he would do – almost – anything for her.

They were going to refurbish the whole of the first floor of the pub and make a grand home for them both. They were going to settle down together. What more could he ask of life?

She had put her bungalow up for sale, and there were already numerous potential buyers. The holiday home idea was still alive, but they had put it on the back burner, decided not to rush into anything. Photos on the internet can be very misleading, gently does it. They had time, the rest of their lives, in fact.

Jennifer was doing her utmost to get Trish out of his life. The divorce proceedings were going ahead and Jennifer knew how to get what she wanted. By God, I`m glad she`s on my side, Toby had often been heard saying. Yes, she`s expensive, but worth every penny. Not like Trish. Whoops, Toby often still fell into the trap of allowing hatred to quell in his breast when he thought of Trish. But he was getting better at dampening it.

He had so much to be happy about, so much to be satisfied with, yes, he was content. No more, he was overjoyed.

He had once caught himself trying to find some catchy phrase for his situation – just like the Six Pack had – and had come up with, the Full House - three of a kind (Jack, Cath and Sadie) and a pair (Rachel and himself).

Somehow, he couldn't quite get Danny into the picture. He was there, he worked hard and reliably, but didn't really want to be a part of anything. Shame, but there you go.

Then again, how fast things can change - Jack and Cath were now settled in the old outbuildings behind the courtyard of the pub. They had found each other and were planning their future together. Sadie was still working at the pub and was in safe hands with Connor. So, he couldn't call it three of a kind anymore anyway, could he?

A Foursome it was to be. A little unfair to Sadie, she was really still part of the parcel, and with Connor, they could have their own Six Pack. Oh my God - he was so obsessed with that damn pack.

What he had was just as good, and with them alongside, it was perfect.

Indeed, they comprised a Full Pack.

Why, he need seek no more.

Miss Mac's Legacy

Ellie MacGuire died without knowing just how successful the Appeal would be. However, she died knowing she had made a lasting mark in her community. With no family members around her, she had dedicated her life to her work and her pupils. On her dying bed, she had chosen Connor, her attentive carer at the hospice, as an agent for her life's work. She had chosen well.

Connor, with the backing of his trusty "Six Pack" and the additional support of "The Woolpack" landlord Toby and his partner, Rachel, initiated:

"The Miss Mac Appeal"

They took on the responsibility to fulfil a promise made to a dying woman and committed themselves to a mission that took them into unknown territory. None of the participants had any past experience with how a donation scheme worked, or how an Appeal could be set up, managed, advertised, and successfully completed. What they did have was faith in themselves, their undertaking, and their cause.

The Appeal started small, and it grew. There was suddenly an awareness in the community which had hitherto been latent. In its first year, the Appeal collected the grand sum of 46,755 pounds and thus enabled all Year 3 pupils of the Woodford Estate Primary School free access to school dinners for a full academic year.

The Appeal sparked further awareness in the Town Hall and discussion soon began as to how the town itself could support the schools in the area, but, as we all know, those windmills grind very slowly.

The Six Pack were justifiably proud of themselves and what they had achieved. Their meetings at the Woolpack were less frequent but remained a constant in their lives. They all looked forward to the get-together on the first Wednesday of each month, an important fixture in their respective calendars.

Encouraged by the success of the Appeal, they (+ their 2 sturdy comrades), decided to continue with their work. It became an annual appeal with donations arriving from local businesses and entrepreneurs, private citizens and school children donating revenues from sponsored events to school fetes. The "Woolpack Sponsored Walk" was soon to be renowned beyond the boundaries of the town, with more and more participants registering every year.

The work behind the Appeal was rewarding, albeit strenuous. All members of the committee, of the administration team and all involved with the organisation of the events could rest assured that they, just like Miss Mac, were making their mark in the community.

Where would we be without such members of society?

"Chapeau"

Rachel's Recipes

Cheesy Ratatouille filling, healthy, & tasty

Ingredients: 400gr mince (beef)
1 tablespoon olive oil
1 medium-sized aubergine (diced)
2 onions (diced)
1 clove garlic (finely chopped)
2 medium-sized courgettes
1 red pepper (sliced)
1 yellow pepper (sliced)
1 can chopped tomatoes
herbes de Provence
salt & pepper
200gr grated cheese

Method:

Heat a coated frying pan and crumble the mince into it. Fry lightly and season with salt and pepper. Remove meat from pan.

Add olive oil to pan and heat. Add onions and garlic and fry slightly. Then add aubergines, courgettes and peppers.

Add tomatoes, a spoonful of herbes de Provence and pinch of salt & pepper. Stir well, cover the pan and leave to cook for 15 – 20 minutes at low heat.

Take pan off the heat, add mince to the vegetables, and mix well. Add a little more of the seasoning and cover the pan. Leave to stand for 5 minutes.

Put all ingredients into an oven dish and sprinkle with grated cheese.

Place in pre-heated oven (175 degrees) and cook for 20 minutes.

Meat Roll with Goat's Cheese Filling and Zaziki continental touch to family eating

Ingredients:

400gr mince (beef)
1 egg
3 tablespoons breadcrumbs
1 pack goat's cheese
Salt, pepper, basil, oregano
1 cucumber
1 clove garlic
1 tablespoon olive oil
Salt, pepper
150gr. Greek joghurt

Method:

Place 400gr mince in a mixing bowl and mix with 1 egg, some salt, some pepper, some basil, and some oregano.

Add enough breadcrumbs (approx. 3 tablespoons) to make the mixture less stodgy and thus more formable.

Take half of the mixture and lay it on the working surface in rectangular form, approx. 1,5 cm thick.

Cut the goat's cheese into slices and lay these on the mince mixture, leaving a margin.

Place the second half of the mixture on top and roll into form.

Pay special attention that the seams are sealed to ensure that no cheese oozes out during cooking.

Place in a pre-heated oven (150 degrees) for 30 minutes

Peel the cucumber and cut into thin slithers. Mix together with the Greek joghurt and add the olive oil, salt, pepper, and garlic to taste.

This all tastes best when served with chips, or tomato rice.

Cottage Pie
the perfect family meal

Ingredients:

2 tablespoons sunflower oil
1 onion, finely chopped
1 celery stalk, finely chopped
1 large carrot, finely chopped
100 gr. peas
400gr mince (beef)
2 teaspoons flour
¼ litre stock (beef)
1 tablespoon tomato purèe
2 tablespoons Worcester sauce
salt, pepper
4 potatoes, peeled & cut
25 gr butter
Milk
salt, pepper, (paprika)
150gr grated cheese

Method:

Heat the oil in a pan and add onion, celery and carrot. Cook for approx. 15 minutes. Add mince, season with salt and pepper, and cook for further 5 minutes, stirring well. Add flour, stock and, tomato purèe, and Worcester sauce, stirring constantly.

Cook potatoes in salted boiling water for approx. 20 minutes. Drain away water.

Cut up potatoes, add butter and enough milk to give a smooth texture whilst stirring. Season with salt and pepper, then mash until soft.

Place the meat/vegetable mixture in an oven dish.

Cover the mixture with the mashed potato and top with grated cheese.

Place in pre-heated oven (approx. 150 degrees) and heat until the cheese has melted.

Sprinkle with paprika and serve immediately.

Stuffed Green Peppers with Rice just that little bit different

Ingredients:

3 green peppers
400gr mince (beef)
1 egg
3 tablespoons breadcrumbs
Salt, pepper, basil, oregano
2 tablespoons cooking oil
2 tablespoons flour
1 beef stock cube
4 tablespoons tomato purèe

Method:

Shell the green peppers and cook in salted, boiling water for 15 minutes.

Remove from the water, but do not drain the water away (needed later for the sauce)

Mix the mince, egg, breadcrumbs and seasoning to a dough-like consistency.

Stuff the meat mixture into the peppers.

To make the sauce, heat cooking oil in a medium-sized saucepan and add the flour, stirring well. Add the crumbled beef stock cube and the tomato purèe and then stir in as much of the left-over "water" to make a smooth sauce.

Place the peppers in the sauce and cook for 20 minutes on medium heat.

Serve with rice.

Potato Lasagne with Mince wrapped in Bacon makes a good impression

Ingredients:

1 onion
400gr mince (beef)
1 tablespoon tomato purèe
Salt, pepper
12 slices bacon
6 medium-sized potatoes
2 tablespoons flour
150gr grated cheese

Method:

Peel and dice the onion, mix 1/3 with the mince and the tomato purèe, then season with salt and pepper.

Place the bacon slices in the medium-sized oven dish, overlapping the sides by approx. 3 centimetres.

Peel and thinly slice the potatoes, mix with the remaining onion and the flour, then season with salt and pepper.

Place ½ the potato mix on the bacon slices in the oven dish and cover with 100gr. cheese.

Layer the mince mix over the cheese and then add a layer of potato mix.

The overlapping bacon is flapped over the potato mix.

Top with remaining cheese.

Cook in a pre-heated oven (175 degrees) for 45 - 50 minutes.

Mince Stew enjoyed best in company

Ingredients: 1 tablespoon cooking oil
400gr mince (beef)
5 medium-sized potatoes
1 red pepper
1 green pepper
2 carrots
1 can (400gr) tomatoes
200gr sour cream
2 tablespoons tomato purèe
1/3 litre vegetable stock
Sugar, salt, paprika

Method:

Peel and cut the potatoes and the carrots into small pieces. Shell the peppers and slice into small pieces.

Heat the cooking oil in a saucepan and crumble the mince into it. Add the can of tomatoes, the tomato purèe, and the vegetable stock. Stir well.

Add the potatoes, the carrots, and the peppers.

Cover and simmer on medium heat for 40 minutes.

Season with salt, a pinch of sugar, and some paprika.

Add the sour cream and stir well.

Serve with freshly baked bread.

www.ingramcontent.com/pod-product-compliance
Lightning Source LLC
Chambersburg PA
CBHW041136110526
44590CB00027B/4038